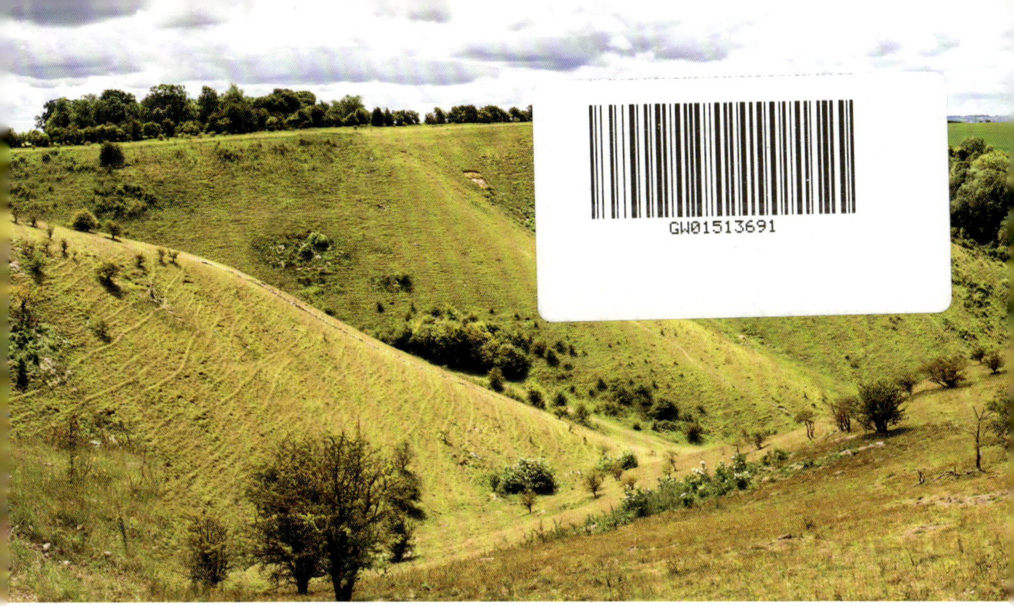

More Great Walks in the Chilterns

Andrew Clark, Richard Bradbury & Colin Drake

Contents

		Miles	PAGE
	Foreword		5
	The Chilterns		6
	Chiltern Society		7
	Information for walkers		8
1	Barton-le-Clay	6.8	9
2	Sundon	4.5	13
3	Lilley	5.6	17
4	Ayot St Lawrence	5.6	21
5	Studham/Whipsnade	5.3	25
6	Gade Valley	4.0	29
7	Hemel Hempstead	6.5	33
8	Ivinghoe/Ashridge	6.0	37
9	Dancersend	5.0	41
10	Cholesbury	6.8	45
11	Princes Risborough	7.2	49
12	Hampden	4.5	53
13	Bledlow	5.0	57
14	Chorleywood – Chesham	8.0	61
15	Rickmansworth	6.0	65
16	Colne Valley	6.2	69
17	W. Wycombe/Hughenden	5.5	73
18	High Wycombe	5.5	77
19	Christmas Common	5.3	81
20	Cookham	4.1	85
21	Nettlebed	5.2	89
22	Nuffield/Swyncombe	5.8	93
23	Checkendon	5.6	97
24	Henley	11.5	101
25	Dorney	5.3	105

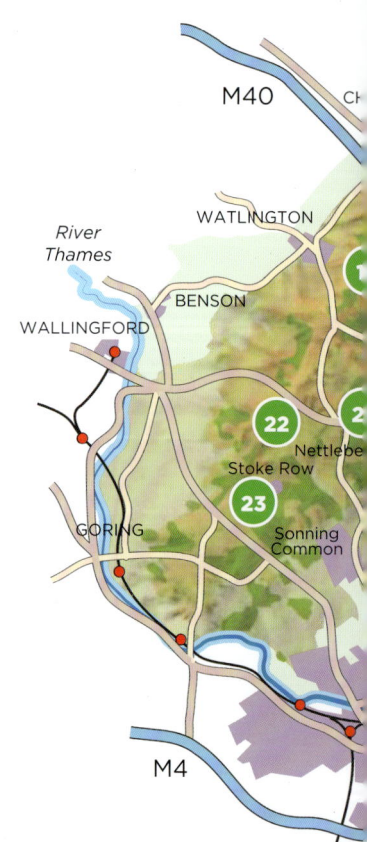

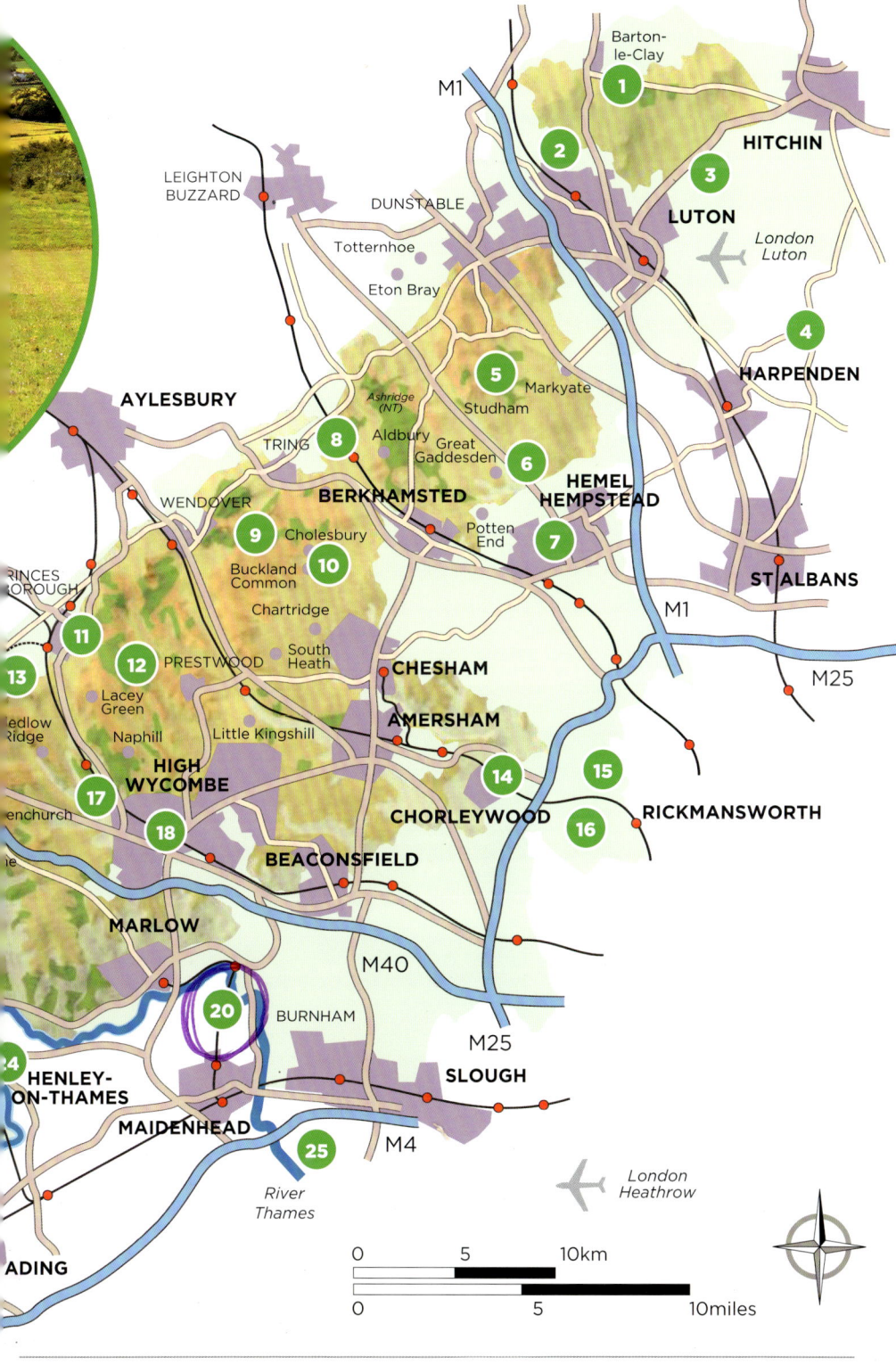

Croxley Common Moor

Foreword

In 2015 the Chiltern Society published *50 Great Walks in the Chilterns*, in celebration of its 50th anniversary. The book has since been widely used by walkers of all ages and abilities keen to explore the best of what the region has to offer in its countryside, villages and towns.

The Chilterns cover a bigger area than many people realise, from the Barton and Pegsdon Hills in the northeast all the way down to the River Thames, and with so many wonderful places to choose from it seemed a shame to stop at a mere 50 walks! We therefore set about devising another 25 which we hope will encourage you to get out into parts of the Chilterns that are new to you, and perhaps even enhance your appreciation of more familiar surroundings. Whether you're striding across the hills, wandering through a beech wood, meandering beside a chalk stream, looking at the wildlife or enjoying some refreshments in a welcoming pub, we're sure you'll agree that the Chilterns deserve their title 'Area of Outstanding Natural Beauty'.

At the same time, it's important to sound a cautionary note. The Chilterns are undoubtedly much loved and attract thousands of visitors every year, but it would be a mistake to assume that their beauty is sacrosanct, or their wellbeing guaranteed. While some development is inevitable, indeed essential, encroachment into the Green Belt for housing, airport expansion and the controversial High Speed Two are just three of the challenges the region currently faces. If you add to them the loss of community facilities such as pubs and local shops, reduced spending on paths and bridleways like those used in these walks, and the danger of the chalk streams drying up, the picture is not as idyllic as it might first appear.

These are serious issues, but please don't let them deter you from taking to the extensive Rights of Way network and sampling these great walks! The routes vary in length, and some require a little more effort than others, but at the beginning of each one we give a brief indication of what you can expect. We also draw your attention to points of interest along the way: these may relate to the landscape, the flora and fauna, the history, the architecture, the people associated with a particular location, or some other feature of the walk that we feel will enrich your experience.

If, as you explore, you find yourself inspired to help care for the Chilterns and preserve the qualities that make them so special, why not join – if you haven't already done so – the growing band of Chiltern Society volunteers? In the meantime, happy walking!

Above: Alford Arms, Frithsden & view from Aldbury Nowers

The Chilterns

The landscape of the Chilterns is varied and full of interest. Much of it is designated an Area of Outstanding Natural Beauty, and there are also Sites of Special Scientific Interest (SSSI). Nature reserves can be found in abundance, including Brush Hill/Whiteleaf Hill, Prestwood and Bottom Wood (all Chiltern Society sites).

When on foot in the Chilterns you may find yourself following ancient routes such as The Ridgeway or The Icknield Way, as well as encountering numerous historic buildings and sites. There are Neolithic burial mounds, such as that on the Chiltern Society's site at Whiteleaf Hill near Princes Risborough; Iron Age hillforts, two fine examples being Boddington Hillfort in Wendover Woods and Cholesbury Camp (another Chiltern Society site); and the fascinating ruins of a Norman motte and bailey castle in Berkhamsted. Churches from several different centuries are also a prominent feature. In more recent times a number of large estates were created, and many of them still survive today in one form or another. During WWI the Chilterns were used to train thousands of recruits, and the remains of practice trenches can still be seen near Berkhamsted and on Whiteleaf Hill.

Furniture manufacturing has played a major role in Chiltern history, its success based on the availability of timber from local forests. The presence of a large amount of clay led to a thriving tile and brick making industry. Clay, chalk and flint are key components of the region's geology, and have had a significant impact on many aspects of Chiltern life through the ages – flint, for example, was fashioned into tools and arrow heads in the Stone Age, then much later used extensively as a building material.

The underlying geology and landform provides the raw base on which the wildlife of the Chilterns has developed. The area exhibits different habitat characteristics, ranging from rolling, open farmland interspersed with copses and hedgerows, through to hilly chalk downland, and dense, predominantly beech woodland with some oak. In the last Ice Age, much of the characteristic scenery of the north Chilterns was formed through the erosion of the chalk plateau, giving rise to the sinuous coombes and sweeping downland hills that provide the recognisable and special landscape. Chalk streams, such as the River Chess, the Gade and the Misbourne offer rare and currently endangered habitats to a variety of species. The chalk grassland is a nationally important habitat for flowers and butterflies in particular. Among those you may see are Chiltern gentians, common spotted, pyramidal and fragrant orchids, chalkhill blue, marbled white and dark green fritillary butterflies, and even the elusive purple pasque flower. The grasslands are also an excellent habitat for insects like grasshoppers and crickets. On a summertime walk after dark you may even chance upon the unmistakeable luminescence of glow-worms.

Birdlife is equally diverse, with a range of species enjoying the insects and small mammals that frequent the open grasslands. Lapwings and skylarks are still a common sight, along with buzzards and meadow pipits, not to mention the seemingly ubiquitous red kites – a major Chiltern success story.

Welcome to the Chilterns!

Chiltern Society

Caring for the Chilterns

Covering four counties and over 650 square miles, the Chilterns is a special place to live, work and explore. The Chiltern Society is the only registered charity dedicated to conserving, celebrating and caring for this unique rural landscape.

With 7,000 members and 500 active volunteers, we:

- Maintain an extensive network of pathways for the enjoyment of walkers, cyclists and horse riders
- Help to provide safe havens for wildlife by improving woodlands, nature reserves and streams across the region, at our own sites and at many others
- Work to protect the landscape from overbearing and damaging development
- Campaign to protect and improve the natural environment for residents and visitors alike
- Celebrate the diverse heritage across the Chilterns by working with historic buildings, museums, landscapes and organisations charged with keeping our heritage alive
- Organise a huge variety of walks, workshops, activities and events to help you and your family discover the best of the Chilterns.

By joining the Chiltern Society you can help make all this work possible and discover what the Chilterns has to offer. You'll also be first to hear about our events, and receive *Chiltern* – our quarterly magazine packed with fascinating articles and great features – delivered directly to your door.

Website: **www.chilternsociety.org.uk** Email: **office@chilternsociety.org.uk** Call: **01494 771250**
Address: **Chiltern Society, White Hill Centre, White Hill, Chesham, Bucks HP5 1AG**

Information for walkers

THE ROUTES

All walks in the book have been thoroughly checked by Chiltern Society members. The routes use public rights of way, recognised permissive paths, roads, or cross public open space. The Chilterns are well walked and the paths well maintained, so route finding should be quite straightforward. If, however, you encounter problems regarding the accuracy of the guidebook or the condition of any paths, please report them to the Chiltern Society on 01494 771250 or email office@chilternsociety.org.uk.

Many walks cross land used for economic purposes such as agriculture, forestry or the rearing of game, so please make every effort to minimise your impact on the day-to-day life of the countryside and follow the Countryside Code at all times. In addition to the summary below, you can find the Code in full at www.naturalengland.org.uk.

THE COUNTRYSIDE CODE

RESPECT
- Other people
- Consider the local community and other people enjoying the outdoors
- Leave gates and property as you find them and follow paths unless wider access is available

PROTECT
- The natural environment
- Leave no trace of your visit and take your litter home
- Keep dogs under effective control

ENJOY
- The outdoors
- Plan ahead and be prepared
- Follow advice and local signs

WALKING CONDITIONS AND EQUIPMENT

Conditions underfoot vary considerably depending on the season and the weather. When dry there are few problems, but if it's been wet some paths may be muddy and/or slippery. In summer there may be overgrown vegetation, such as nettles or brambles. Please ensure that you choose suitable clothing and footwear, and take note of the latest weather forecast. It's worth remembering that although the Chiltern Hills are modest in height, the weather on the higher ground can differ markedly from the surrounding plains, and usually not in a good way! There are areas where the mobile phone signal is still patchy, so it's advisable not to be too reliant on your phone as a way of organising your lift home at the end of the day, for example.

PARKING AND PUBLIC TRANSPORT

Details of possible parking places are given in the introductory information to each walk, along with details of any relevant public transport available at the time of writing. Where space is limited, please park considerately.

MAPS

Although we hope that the maps in the book will be sufficient for you to follow the walks as described and identify points of interest without difficulty, we suggest that you also take with you the appropriate Ordnance Survey or Chiltern Society maps, in case you wish to deviate from the recommended route for any reason. You may also wish to download ViewRanger GPS, an exciting app that allows you to access trails, maps and walking routes from your smartphone or tablet. It enables you to view your position on a detailed map and use the navigation system to follow routes, with no need for a phone signal or mobile data. You can record your track as you go and create a record of your adventure. Enriched with descriptions, local information and photographs, ViewRanger is a great aid for exploring the Chilterns.

WALK 1

Views from the Barton Hills

This walk starts by criss-crossing the border between Herts and Central Beds, before climbing up the Chilterns escarpment. It then passes a hidden hillfort, meets three major walking routes and provides magnificent views over the surrounding countryside.

> *Though the hill is high, I still desire to walk up it. I don't care how difficult it is, because I understand that it leads to the way of life.*
> — JOHN BUNYAN

LENGTH: 6.8 miles/11km

TERRAIN: A moderate stile-free walk on good surfaces, but can be muddy at times. There are a number of gates to pass through. One climb out of Hexton and a total ascent of 140m/460ft

START & FINISH: St Nicholas Church, Church Road, Barton-le-Clay MK45 4LA. Grid ref: TL 085 304

FOOD & DRINK: Pubs and cafés in Barton-le-Clay. The Raven pub and Lavender Tearooms in Hexton

MAPS: OS Explorer 193, Chiltern Society 25 & 26

PARKING: Church Rd, Barton-le-Clay MK45 4LA

LOCAL TRANSPORT: Bus 81 runs between Luton and Bedford, and Bus 79 between Luton and Shefford, both from Monday to Saturday. Full details can be found on www.travelinesoutheast.org.uk

Views from the Barton Hills

St Nicholas Church

THE ROUTE

Walk back down Church Road to the junction and bear right over Hexton Road into Manor Road. Walk along for 500m past Ramsey Manor School to a surfaced path on the right just before 109 Manor Road.

1 Turn right along the path, go over the footbridge and follow the left-hand field edge. Where the hedgerow on the left ends, continue straight ahead across the field. Follow the path as it turns to the left then the right, and keep to the hedgerow on the right for a further 500m to cross a footbridge. Bear right over the field to a lane.

2 Turn right along the lane to a T-junction. Turn right, walk past The Raven pub and Hexton village hall and on to reach the junction with a major road (Barton Road). Cross to the road opposite and walk along it for 200m to a path on the right.

3 Bear right past an automatic gate along a wide rough track. Where the track swings to the right, continue straight ahead up the steep grassy path and along to the edge of a field. Stay in the same direction along its right-hand edge into the next field.

4 Turn right for a few metres and then left, keeping to the left of the hedgerow, to a road. Turn right along the road for 160m and left through the entrance to Mortgrove Farm. Walk along the surfaced driveway, go through the metal gate and past the white building on the left. Where that ends, carry straight on through a gate and continue along the right-hand edge of the field. Pass under the overhead cables and, where the hedgerow on the right ends, continue ahead for about 50m to a junction with a major path.

5 This path is part of The Icknield and Chiltern Ways and the John Bunyan Trail. Turn right along it, go past the green posts on either side and continue for a further 250m to the next major junction.

Barton-le-Clay

WALK 1

6 Turn right along the right-hand field edge, pass under the same line of overhead cables to a road. Turn right along the road for 150m to a path on the left signposted for the Barton Hills.

7 Turn left, go through the wooden barrier and walk through the wood to a farm track and the entrance to Barton Hill Farm. Continue in the same direction along the farm track for 800m to a gate on the left into the Barton Hills National Nature Reserve (NNR).

8 Turn left through the gate and immediately right along the ridge. Keeping to the left of the fence, go through a gate before descending towards the church in Barton-le-Clay. Go through the next gate. Walk down a series of steps and through the last gate into a field. Bear left round the field edge to a lane. Turn right along it into Church Lane to finish the walk.

Views from the Barton Hills

POINTS OF INTEREST

BARTON-LE-CLAY was known as Barton in the Clay until the 1960s, and got its name from its position on a ridge of gault clay. The manor is mentioned in the Domesday Book as being under the ownership of Ramsey Abbey. St Nicholas Church is a Grade I listed building that has played a central role in the life of the village for 800 years.

Ⓐ HEXTON The parish of Hexton is in Hertfordshire, but is surrounded on three sides by Central Bedfordshire. It's designated Green Belt. There's been a settlement since Saxon times. In the early 20th century the village was redeveloped as a 'model village'. Notable buildings include Hexton Manor, a Grade II listed country house and gardens, Grange Hall, a Grade II listed building, and The Raven pub.

Ⓑ RAVENSBURGH CASTLE is an Iron Age hillfort, hidden among the trees on the hillside. It's regarded as the best example of a pre-Roman camp in Hertfordshire. The workings consist of a large, nearly oval enclosure, covering 16 1/2 acres, or, with its defences, 22 acres. It's protected on the east and south sides by a rampart and ditch. The defences on the west side have a second rampart and ditch. The north side has an inner rampart, beyond which are two sloping platforms and two shallow banks, with a small outer ditch. The main entrance, which is about 90ft wide, is at the northwest angle, where a neck of land joins the plateau to the body of the hill. Limited excavations during the 1960s showed that it was built about 400 BC and refortified in about 50 BC. It's been suggested that it might have been the headquarters of the Celtic chieftain Cassivelaunus, attacked in 54 BC, possibly by Julius Caesar.

Ⓒ MEETING OF THREE TRAILS *The Icknield Way* is one of Britain's most important ancient tracks, said to be the oldest road in Britain. It predates the Romans and may have extended from Norfolk all the way to the Devon coast. It's one of the four ancient highways of England mentioned by Geoffrey of Monmouth. First used in Neolithic times by flint traders, it's now a 120ml/195km long distance path.

John Bunyan Trail In his early years Bunyan lived in Elstow, near Bedford, and travelled widely in the local area, first as an itinerant tinker and later as a non-conformist preacher. He was imprisoned for nearly 12 years in Bedford Gaol, where he began his masterpiece, *The Pilgrim's Progress.* The trail visits the places where Bunyan preached and which formed the inspiration for the landscape in the book.

The Chiltern Way was set up as a millennium project by Chiltern Society volunteers. It's a circular walking route of 134 miles with two optional extensions and an additional loop taking the total route to a maximum of 220 miles. A new guidebook for the trail was published in 2017. See www.chilternsociety.org.uk.

Ⓓ BARTON HILLS NNR This reserve has been designated a Site of Site of Special Scientific Interest (SSSI). It's a chalk downland site with a large population of rare flowers including the pasque flower, greater pignut and fleawort. There are also considerable numbers of chalkhill blue, marbled white and grizzled skipper butterflies. The Barton Hills are also thought to have been the inspiration for Bunyan's Celestial Mountains in *The Pilgrim's Progress.*

This walk was created with the assistance of John Pearce, a local Chiltern Society member and John Gover, an active member of The Chess Valley Archaeological and Historical Society.

NEARBY CHILTERN SOCIETY WALKS

SUNDON HILLS COUNTRY PARK – Walk 2 of this book passes close by at Sharpenhoe Clappers.

LILLEY AND THE GALLEY & WARDEN HILLS – Walk 3 of this book meets the route at Waypoint 6.

BARTON-LE-CLAY – Walk 6 of the *50 Great Walks in the Chilterns* book meets this walk near the entrance to Barton Hills NNR.

Sundon Hills Country Park

WALK 2

A short and easy walk that's attractive at any time of year. Once you've entered the Country Park the rest of the route is quiet and peaceful, with magnificent views looking north into Bedfordshire and beyond. There's a longer option which visits the Iron Age hillfort at Sharpenhoe Clappers.

It is always hard to see the purpose in wilderness wanderings until after they are over.
JOHN BUNYAN

LENGTH: 4.5 miles/7.2km, with a longer 6.2 mile/10km option

TERRAIN: An easy stile-free walk on good surfaces. There are a number of kissing gates. Both walks descend a steep set of steps and have one steep climb. The main walk has a total ascent of 130m/430ft, the longer option 180m/590ft

START & FINISH: The Red Lion, 13 Harlington Road, Sundon LU3 3PE. Grid ref: TL 045 277

FOOD & DRINK: The Red Lion. None on route

MAPS: OS Explorer 193, Chiltern Society 25

PARKING: The Red Lion have given permission for their car park to be used. They would be delighted to offer you refreshments. There's also a car park at the Country Park (Waypoint 1)

LOCAL TRANSPORT: Bus 78 runs between Luton and Upper Sundon, Mondays to Saturdays. Full details can be found on www.travelinesoutheast.org.uk

13

Sundon Hills Country Park

View from Sundon Hills Country Park

THE ROUTE

Turn left out of the pub car park and walk along Harlington Road. Just after the junction with Streatley Road, climb onto the grass verge on the left and continue in the same direction out of the village. Follow the verge round the left-hand bend and stay on it for 200m, then cross to the opposite side of the road. Stay in the same direction for a further 300m to the entrance of Sundon Hills Country Park.

1 Turn right through the car park and the gate at the end onto the hillside. Take time to enjoy the magnificent views to the north. Continue in the same direction to the left of the hedgerow for 650m and go through a gate on the right at the far corner. Follow the path ahead as it first bends to the left then the right, and turn right through a gate waymarked for The Chiltern Way, The Icknield Way and the John Bunyan Trail.

2 Continue straight ahead on a path between fields and at the end turn left along a path to the left of a wood. Where that ends bear left on a stony track, and when that peters out turn right and walk along the top of the field to the corner. Follow the field round to the left. After 100m turn right into the wood and immediately left down to a path junction. *The optional longer route starts here.*

3 Keep straight on down a set of steep steps to a path junction at the bottom. Continue ahead to descend into a field. Follow the hedgerow on the right for 400m and bear right over a concrete footbridge into the next field.

4 Turn immediately left along the field edge to join a wide track. Stay in the same direction past a wood and lake on the right, and continue on the main farm track to meet a lane. Turn left along the lane to a permissive path on the left just before the T-junction at Sundon Road.

5 Go through the gate, follow the path between the fields and pass through a gate up into a wood. Turn right at a path junction and walk along the edge of the wood. Go through a gate, pass an information board and turn left up two sets of steps, through a gate and into a field.

6 Turn right and follow the fence uphill. Where that ends, bear right uphill to a gate at the top. Go through it, and the one on the right, to a road. Cross, then turn right along the verge and left into a field. Follow the hedgerow on the left to the end of the field. Turn right downhill and left through a gap into the next field. Bear diagonally left over the field to the rough track by the sewage works. Turn left and follow it for a further 400m to return to the pub.

OPTIONAL LONGER ROUTE

Turn right up the slope and, after 300m, follow the path to the right then left out of the wood. Continue for a further 300m to where the path turns right and go through the gate directly ahead into a field.

7 Cross, go through the gate and down the steps to a road. Walk through the car park and a gate and along a surfaced path into The National Trust's (NT) Sharpenhoe site. Go past the information board, stay on the surfaced track for 240m and turn left on The Chiltern Way. This turning is just before the surfaced track climbs and turns sharply left. Follow the wide track through the woods and up the steps onto a grassy slope. Stay in the same direction, keeping to the right of the fence for 530m to reach the end of the wood and the top of a set of steps. Descend the steps to the edge of a field at the bottom.

8 Turn immediately left under the overhead cables and go through two gates into a field. Turn left, follow the fence on the left, then stay in the same direction across the field to leave by a gate into a lane. Cross to the bridleway opposite and follow the wide track along the field edge for 630m to a major path junction at the entrance to the NT's Moleskin and Markham Hills site. Do not enter – instead turn right downhill, follow the field edge round to the right and go left through a gap in the hedgerow into a field to rejoin the main route at Waypoint 4.

Sundon Hills Country Park

POINTS OF INTEREST

UPPER SUNDON The parish of Sundon is made up of both Upper and Lower Sundon. The names comes from the Old English *Sunna's Dun* or 'Hill of a man called Sunna'. At the time of the Domesday Book there was one entry showing that William d'Eu held the manor, which was valued at 10 hides. In Lower Sundon is the 13th century St Mary's Church. Almost opposite The Red Lion is the old Methodist church, which was erected in 1847 and rebuilt in 1913. John Wesley, the preacher and theologian who co-founded Methodism, is said to have visited the area on a number of occasions. Behind the bus stop is Bright's Pond, which was used by farmers to wash their carts after returning from the fields. It has an interesting information board.

A **SUNDON HILLS COUNTRY PARK** belongs to Central Bedfordshire Council and is managed in partnership with the NT. It's one of the highest points in the county and also a Site of Special Scientific Interest. The Park is mostly on a north-facing escarpment of lower chalk and unimproved grassland. The site is important for many species of flora and fauna, including such plants as the fly orchid, as well as pyramidal, common spotted and bee orchids. It also has sanicle, a relatively unusual umbellifer of beech woods.

B **JOHN BUNYAN TRAIL, THE ICKNIELD WAY & THE CHILTERN WAY** all meet on this walk. The John Bunyan Trail is a 75 mile circular route that starts and finishes in the Country Park. It visits many of the sites connected with John Bunyan, puritan evangelist and author of *The Pilgrim's Progress*. For more information about all three trails, see Walk 1.

C **SHARPENHOE CLAPPERS** is ancient woodland and chalk downland owned by the NT. The name Sharpenhoe comes from 'sharp spur of land'. There seems to be some debate over the name 'Clappers'. Some think it derives from the medieval Latin term *claperius*, meaning a heap of stones or rabbit hole, others believe it comes from the French for rabbit warren. The site contains an Iron Age hillfort and is covered in beech trees.

This walk was created with the help of Nigel Seabrooke, a Chiltern Society walker.

NEARBY CHILTERN SOCIETY WALKS
VIEWS FROM THE BARTON HILLS – Walk 1 of this book is nearby.
BARTON-LE-CLAY – Walk 6 of the *50 Great Walks in the Chilterns* book meets this route at the top of the steps just before descending to Waypoint 8.

Lilley and the Galley & Warden Hills

WALK 3

A wonderful walk starting from the historic village of Lilley and passing through some of the best chalk grassland in the Chiltern Hills. It also touches on three major walking trails.

LENGTH: 5.6 miles/9km, with a shorter 4.9 mile/7.9km option

TERRAIN: Easy walking on good paths and wide bridleways with two short, steep climbs. Fairly exposed in bad weather. Stile-free but numerous gates. Total ascent 150m/500ft or 120m/400ft on the shorter option

START & FINISH: West Street, Lilley LU2 8LN, Grid ref: TL 118 264

FOOD & DRINK: The Lilley Arms. None on route

MAPS: OS Explorer 193, Chiltern Society 25 & 30

PARKING: Lilley Arms car park if you're using the pub, otherwise roadside in West Street. Be sure to leave plenty of space for large agricultural vehicles

LOCAL TRANSPORT: Bus 101 runs between Luton and Stevenage all week and stops in the village 200m from Waypoint 1 of the walk. Full details can be found on www.travelinesoutheast.org.uk

Lilley and the Galley & Warden Hills

Approaching Galley Hill

View towards Luton

THE ROUTE

From the car park, turn right past the pub and the grass triangle to the road junction. Cross, bear right along the pavement past the church for 160m to the entrance to the Cassel Memorial Hall and turn right into its car park. The route will now follow The Chiltern Way for the next 3.5 miles.

1 Walk past the hall, take the path to the right of the white lion emblem and continue ahead for 100m to enter a field. Stay in the same direction along the right-hand edge for 750m, go through a small copse and straight across the field ahead. Follow the path over the top of the hill and on to a kissing gate. Go through it into the next field and, staying in same general direction, bear slightly left across the middle to the next gate and a lane.

2 Turn right along the lane for 40m and fork left on a very wide bridleway with concrete tracks. Go past a metal barrier and stay on the track for a further 330m to meet a 4-way junction of bridleways. Continue straight ahead between the hedgerow and field and, where the hedgerow on the left ends, bear left on a wide grassy bridleway between fields. Follow it to the right of the hedgerow as it drops down and then sweeps right up to a kissing gate. Go through it and turn immediately left on a path following the edge of a wood for 250m to a path on the right, just before a set of steps.

3 Turn right uphill, go over a crossing path and climb steeply through the wood to emerge onto the open hillside. Continue uphill, ignore the path bearing left and stay in the same direction to near the top of the hill. Turn left to enjoy the wonderful views over Luton and the surrounding area. To rejoin the main route, bear right uphill and go through a gate at the top. Stay in the same direction to the left of a fence for 400m, passing the triangulation point on the right, and go through the next gate. Continue to follow the path round the hill and down to a fork. Do not take the footpath on the left that descends to a gate, but stay on the path round to the right and

WALK 3

[Map of walk route around Lilley, showing waypoints 1-6, Icknield Way, Galley Hill, Warden Hill, John Bunyan Trail, Chiltern Way, Ward's Wood, Wardswood Lane, George's Plantation, Lilleypark Plantation, Jamaica Plantation, Whitehill Wood, Whitehill Farm, Oaket Wood, Beechill Plantation, Beech Hill, Butterfield Green Road, South Bedfordshire Golf Club, Ward's Farm, Church Farm, Ralphs Farm, Bus stops, A505, directions to A6 (Barton Road), Hitchin, Luton. Scale: 0 to 1km / ½ mile.]

head down to a kissing gate. Go through it to a bridleway and turn right uphill for 130m past the entrance on the left to the Galley and Warden Hills local nature reserve. *The optional shorter route starts here.*

4 A few metres after the entrance turn left on a wide bridleway. Continue along the ridge, ignore the gate on the left and follow the path for a further 180m to where the track swings to the right. Stay straight ahead through a gate and follow the path as it drops down through the next gate to the edge of a golf course. Go straight over the fairway and to the right of a green to meet a rough track. Turn left along it for 50m to reach a wide bridleway on The Icknield Way.

5 Turn right along the bridleway for 300m to a major crossing track and right again to join the John Bunyan Trail. After 800m, look for a path on the right where the John Bunyan Trail leaves this route and the optional shorter route rejoins.

6 Continue in the same direction for a further 1km, passing a wood on the left. The track drops down to the end of the wood and turns right. Continue to follow the track for 120m and, where it bears left, stay straight ahead on a grassy byway towards Lilley. At the surfaced lane, turn right uphill and along to finish the walk at The Lilley Arms.

OPTIONAL SHORTER ROUTE A few metres after the entrance continue straight ahead along the field edge for 1km to a major path junction at Waypoint 6 of the walk. Turn right to rejoin the main route.

The Lilley Arms

19

Lilley and the Galley & Warden Hills

POINTS OF INTEREST

LILLEY is a beautiful village set in stunning countryside. Many of the buildings are at least 250 years old, but the area has been inhabited for much longer. It was recorded as Lillei in the Domesday Book, with 19 villagers, 6 smallholders, 6 slaves and 4 cottagers. St Peter's Church dates from the 12th century, but was rebuilt in 1871 using some of the old fittings. The manor of Lilley dates back before William the Conqueror. It passed through many hands before being conveyed to Thomas Docwra who lived nearby at Putteridge Bury. In 1788, the manor was sold to John Sowerby Esquire, a wealthy merchant of Hatton Garden. The lion from his crest can still be seen on many Lilley cottages – how many can you spot? You'll see the large crest from the closed Silver Lion pub next to the village hall.

A NORTH CHILTERN TRAIL/CHILTERN WAY
The Chiltern Way is a circular trail around the Chilterns Area of Outstanding Natural Beauty, designed by the Chiltern Society (for more information see Walk 1). In 2014 the Society added the North Chiltern Trail, a 43 mile circuit of the best scenery in the north-eastern corner of the Chilterns.

B GALLEY & WARDEN HILLS These hills were Luton Borough Council's first nature reserve. They are one of the most important areas of chalk downland in Bedfordshire and are home to a wide range of wild flowers, many of which will only live on the thin, poor soils. These flowers in turn attract over 20 different butterflies. In summer look out for wild orchids and chalkhill blue and marbled white butterflies. The hills are also rich in history. Running below them are Dray's Ditches, which are the remains of a substantial boundary earthwork first constructed in the Bronze Age. Galley Hill has two Bronze Age barrows. Although these are barely visible today, in the Middle Ages a gallows was built on one of them. Its height guaranteed it was seen by all the local people as a way of deterring them from committing crimes. The Luton magistrates ordered that the bodies of executed criminals should be soaked in tar for three days, before being bound in chains and hoisted onto the gibbet. This was to ensure the bodies would swing in the wind for months before they rotted.

C THE ICKNIELD WAY For more information see Walk 1.

D JOHN BUNYAN TRAIL There were several Dissenters' houses in Lilley. One of these had a cellar where Bunyan could hide to preach in secret. See Walk 1 for more information about Bunyan and the trail.

This walk was created with the assistance of Louis Upton, Chiltern Society Area Footpath Secretary in Luton and Central Bedfordshire.

NEARBY CHILTERN SOCIETY WALKS
VIEWS FROM THE BARTON HILLS – Walk 1 of this book passes close by, along Barton Hill Road.
BARTON-LE-CLAY – Walk 6 of the *50 Great Walks in the Chilterns* book meets this walk near the entrance to Barton Hills National Nature Reserve.

Ayot St Lawrence

WALK 4

A walk which explores the landscape and history of this special corner of Hertfordshire. It starts and finishes in Kimpton and includes two 12th century churches, a neoclassical church, a park designed by Capability Brown and the house of a famous playwright and author.

> *After all, the wrong road always leads somewhere.*
> — GEORGE BERNARD SHAW

LENGTH: 5.6 miles/9km

TERRAIN: A moderate walk on good surfaces. Two modest climbs with a total ascent of 120m/400ft. There are a number of gates and one stile

START & FINISH: The War Memorial, High Street, Kimpton SG4 8RB. Grid ref: TL 175 183

FOOD & DRINK: Cafés and pubs in Kimpton, and The Brocket Arms in Ayot St Lawrence

MAPS: OS Explorer 182, Chiltern Society 29

PARKING: Roadside parking along the High Street, Kimpton SG4 8PT

LOCAL TRANSPORT: Bus 44/45 runs between Luton and Stevenage, Monday to Saturday; Bus 304 runs between Hitchin and St Albans, Monday to Saturday; and Bus 315 runs between Kimpton and Welwyn Garden City, Monday to Friday. Full details can be found on www.travelinesoutheast.org.uk

Leaving Kimpton

Ayot St Lawrence

St Lawrence Church

River Mimram

THE ROUTE

From the war memorial, walk along the High Street to the Dacre Rooms and turn left up Church Lane.

1 Go through the entrance to the parish church of St Peter & St Paul, take the gravel path to the right of it and leave by a gate at the back onto a road. Turn left up the road for 140m and, on the 'S' bend, turn right along a surfaced access road for 1km to reach Hoo Park Cottage.

2 Turn right through a gate to join The Hertfordshire Way. Ignoring the path bearing right, continue straight across the field and along the left-hand side of a wood. Go through a gate, stay to the left-hand edge of two fields, through the next gate and drop down to leave the field by the gate in the bottom left-hand corner. Turn right along the surfaced driveway, go over the stone bridge and continue to a road.

3 Turn right and immediately right again to follow a wide bridleway. On the right is the River Mimram. Continue along the bridleway for 500m to a white painted cottage on the right. Turn right for a short diversion to the old buildings of Rye-end Farm. Return to the cottage, turn right to rejoin the route and stay on this track to a lane. Turn right along the lane past the old watercress beds to a road junction by Kimpton Mill. Turn right and immediately left uphill on Bridleway 38 towards Abbotshay.

4 Follow the bridleway for 1km to reach a lane (Tanyard Lane) and turn right along it for 120m past Abbotshay Farm to a junction. Turn left and follow the bridleway past Ayot Manor House and Ayot House on the right to a road.

5 Turn right past The Brocket Arms pub and the old church, then follow the road round to the left to the junction with Bibbs Hall Lane. Turn right into it. The National Trust property, Shaw's Corner, is to the left. Continue along the lane and, at the left-hand bend, turn immediately right through a gate into a field.

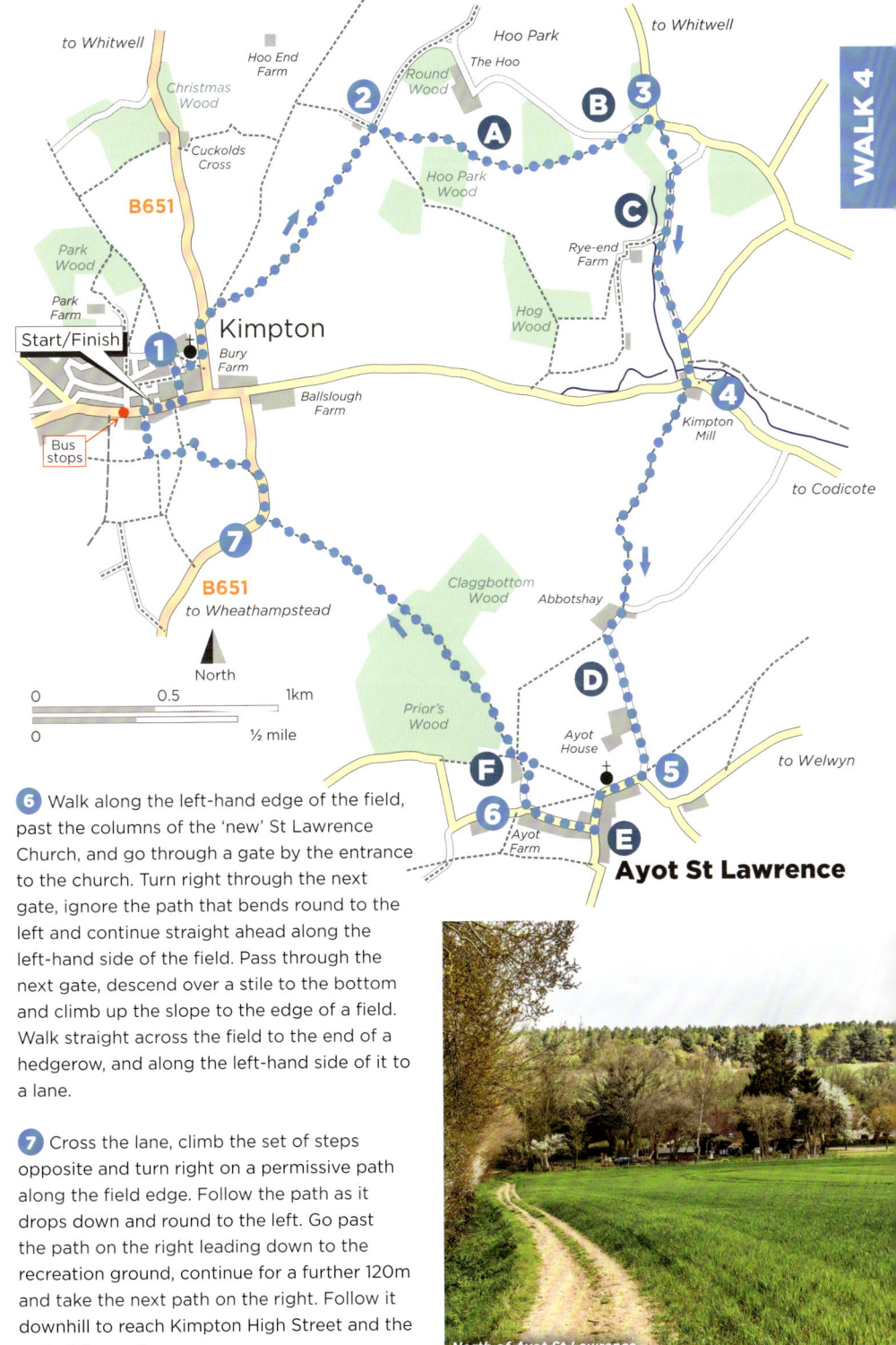

6 Walk along the left-hand edge of the field, past the columns of the 'new' St Lawrence Church, and go through a gate by the entrance to the church. Turn right through the next gate, ignore the path that bends round to the left and continue straight ahead along the left-hand side of the field. Pass through the next gate, descend over a stile to the bottom and climb up the slope to the edge of a field. Walk straight across the field to the end of a hedgerow, and along the left-hand side of it to a lane.

7 Cross the lane, climb the set of steps opposite and turn right on a permissive path along the field edge. Follow the path as it drops down and round to the left. Go past the path on the right leading down to the recreation ground, continue for a further 120m and take the next path on the right. Follow it downhill to reach Kimpton High Street and the end of the walk.

Ayot St Lawrence

POINTS OF INTEREST

Shaw's Corner

KIMPTON is derived from the Saxon *Cyma-tun*, meaning 'homestead of a person called Cyma'. Over the centuries the name went through many changes including Kamintone, Kemytone and Kempton before becoming Kimpton. Along the High Street there are houses dating back to the 16th century, but most in the village are from the 19th and 20th centuries. The oldest building is the Grade I listed St Peter & St Paul Church, which dates from the 12th century. It started with a simple nave and a small chancel, built round the previous wooden church. The oldest bell in the tower dates from the 1300s.

A HOO ESTATE The walk passes through the grounds of the Hoo Estate. The name comes from the family who were lords of the manor from the 13th century, before passing it to the Keates in the 17th century. They built a grand manor house which was eventually demolished in 1958. In 1758 Capability Brown was paid £150 to landscape the grounds, and he created a lake, wooded belts and woodland walks. Much of the Estate has now been returned to agricultural use.

B STONE BRIDGE This bridge once stood over the River Mimram, which has since been diverted. It was designed by Sir William Chambers and built in c1764. It's made from Portland stone and was restored in 2004. It's Grade II listed and a scheduled ancient monument.

C THE MIMRAM is a chalk stream which rises near Whitwell and flows 12 miles to meet the River Lea in Hertford. It inspired Stevie Smith, the poet and novelist, to write her poem *The River God*. On the walk there's a short diversion to the 16th century, Grade II listed Rye-end Farm, which was once part of the Kimpton Hoo Estate. The farm was known for its osier beds, where willow was planted to make baskets. Further down is Kimpton Mill, which used to be a watermill.

D AYOT MANOR HOUSE was once owned by Sir William Parr, brother of Catherine Parr, Henry VIII's last Queen. Ayot House is a Grade II listed house, park and garden, and was once famous as Britain's only silk farm. It was also home to the King and Queen of Romania.

E AYOT ST LAWRENCE is a delightful village with many interesting buildings, including: The Brocket Arms, originally the monastic quarters for the Norman church and said to be haunted by a hanged priest; the old St Lawrence Church, built in about 1150 AD, which was once the parish church but is now in ruins. It was partially demolished in 1775 by Sir Lionel Lyde, who replaced it with the new church; and Shaw's Corner, which was the home of playwright George Bernard Shaw from 1906 until his death in 1950. Today it's owned by the National Trust, and remains much as he left it.

F THE 'NEW' ST LAWRENCE CHURCH is an 18th century neoclassical church, commissioned by Sir Lionel Lyde and designed by Nicholas Revett. It was completed in 1778 on land owned by Lyde, who lived in Ayot House.

Studham & Whipsnade

WALK 5

There's a lot of lovely, rolling countryside in and around Studham Common, and dramatic views from the longer option at Dunstable Downs. This walk visits a tree cathedral and a 16th century church, and offers the possibility of spotting exotic animals at Whipsnade Zoo.

OPTIONAL EXTENSION TO DUNSTABLE DOWNS

The Windcatcher, Dunstable Downs

LENGTH: 5.3 miles/8.5km, with a longer 7.5 mile/12km option

TERRAIN: An easy, stile-free walk on good surfaces which can be muddy at times. There are a number of kissing gates. No steep climbs. A total ascent of 100m/300ft on the main walk and 150m/500ft on the longer option

START & FINISH: Studham War Memorial, on the corner of Church Road and Clement End Road, Studham LU6 2QG. Grid ref: TL 022 158. An alternative start point is The Chilterns Gateway Centre, Dunstable Road, Whipsnade LU6 2GY. Grid ref: TL 007 195

FOOD & DRINK: Studham – The Red Lion in Church Rd LU6 2QA and The Bell in Dunstable Rd LU6 2QG. In Whipsnade the walk passes close to the Old Hunters Lodge, The Cross Roads LU6 2LN. On the longer option there is The Chilterns Gateway Centre

MAPS: OS Explorer 182, Chiltern Society 20 & 21

PARKING: Small car park at the junction of Kensworth Road and Clement End Road LU6 2QG. Grid ref: TL 023 157. If this is full, park in Church Road

LOCAL TRANSPORT: Details for bus services to Studham, Whipsnade and Dunstable Downs can be found on www.travelinesoutheast.org.uk

Studham & Whipsnade

Whipsnade

View from Dunstable Downs

THE ROUTE

From the memorial turn left up Church Road and take the path on the right just after the Methodist church. Walk along the edge of the first field for 350m to a path junction.

1 Turn right along the edge of the same field and the next, and go through a gate onto a road (Dunstable Road). Cross, turn left along the pavement and take the path on the right just after No.132. Walk up through the wood, stay in the same direction between the fields and follow the path along the edge of a housing estate. Continue alongside the next field and pass more houses on the left to drop down to a path junction.

2 Cross over onto the path that runs parallel to the road on the right, and follow it for 400m before turning left up into an estate. Turn right along the pavement, take the path on the right immediately after No.11 Bramblewood, and follow it along the field edge to reach a busy road. Cross the road, turn left along it for 50m and turn right through a kissing gate into the field. Walk along the left-hand edge of the first field and stay in the same direction to go through the gate into the grounds of St Mary Magdalene Church, Whipsnade. Walk past the church and leave the grounds at the front gate onto Whipsnade Green. *The optional longer route starts here.*

3 Turn immediately left and cross the wide, grassy area to a road. Cross over to a rough lane to the left of Chapel Cottage and continue ahead to visit the Tree Cathedral.

4 After exploring the site return to Chapel Cottage, bear right over the road to the lane opposite and walk past Maple Cottage and The Old Post Office to drop down the grassy slope to a lane (Studham Lane). Turn left along it for 600m to reach a path on the right just before the second set of barriers.

5 Take this path, signed for The Chiltern Way,

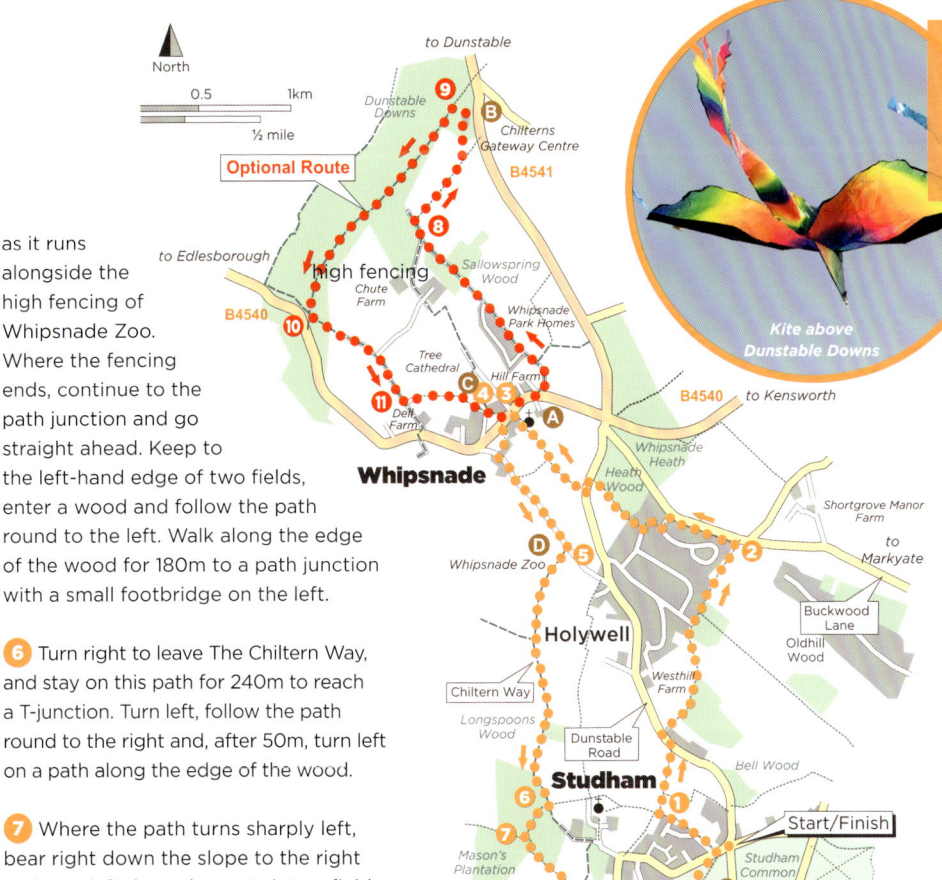

Kite above Dunstable Downs

as it runs alongside the high fencing of Whipsnade Zoo. Where the fencing ends, continue to the path junction and go straight ahead. Keep to the left-hand edge of two fields, enter a wood and follow the path round to the left. Walk along the edge of the wood for 180m to a path junction with a small footbridge on the left.

6 Turn right to leave The Chiltern Way, and stay on this path for 240m to reach a T-junction. Turn left, follow the path round to the right and, after 50m, turn left on a path along the edge of the wood.

7 Where the path turns sharply left, bear right down the slope to the right and turn left through a gate into a field. Go straight on along the path and follow the line of the overhead cables. Stay in the same direction through the gate and over a lane to the bridleway opposite. Continue past a school and onto the wide grassy path to return to the start.

OPTIONAL LONGER ROUTE

Bear half-right over the grass towards a pair of national speed limit signs. Cross the road onto a wide verge and follow the hedgerow round to the left to join a bridleway. Stay straight ahead for 1km to a path junction at the communication mast.

8 Turn right, then right again along the surfaced access road and walk to the Chilterns Gateway Centre.

9 Walk down from the Centre to the Windcatcher sculpture. Turn left along the top of the ridge and to the right of the hedgerow. Go through a gate, continue in the same direction to the left of the pylons for 1km and go through a gate.

10 Bear round to the left on a wide bridleway heading away from the ridge. Continue along the track for 600m to a wooden barrier just after a bungalow on the left.

11 Turn left past the barrier and through a gate into a field. Follow the hedgerow on the right through two more gates into Whipsnade Tree Cathedral to rejoin the main walk at Waypoint 4.

Studham & Whipsnade

POINTS OF INTEREST

STUDHAM is an ancient village referred to in the Domesday Book as Estodham. For many years the parish straddled the border between Bedfordshire and Hertfordshire and was partitioned until 1894, when it was united under Bedfordshire. According to a local story, the Government ruled that whichever council installed electricity first could lay claim to the whole village. There are two pubs: The Bell, which is the highest pub in Bedfordshire and The Red Lion, which used to have a cockfighting pit.

A ST MARY MAGDALENE CHURCH is a simple structure, built of brick, with a 16th century tower, a nave (1719) designed by Nicholas Hawksmoor, and an apse added in 1860. The pulpit and altar rail are Jacobean. The interior is light and well maintained.

Walkers in Studham Lane

B DUNSTABLE DOWNS is a Site of Special Scientific Interest (SSSI) and is renowned for its abundant plants and wildlife. At 243m it's the highest point in Bedfordshire and is a popular venue for gliding, hang gliding, paragliding and kite flying. The Downs played their part in naval history. In the early 19th century they were the site of a signalling station that allowed the Royal Navy to send messages from London to its base in Great Yarmouth. The Chilterns Gateway Centre was built some years ago and has become a very popular meeting place. The Windcatcher aerates the Centre, keeping it cool in summer.

C WHIPSNADE TREE CATHEDRAL was planted in the early 1930s by Edmond Blyth as an act of 'faith, hope and reconciliation' in honour of those killed in WWI. Its design was inspired by Blyth's visit to Liverpool Cathedral. There are grass avenues lined with deciduous and evergreen trees and shrub species, which form the chancel, nave, transepts, chapels and cloisters. The site is owned by the National Trust and administered by the Trustees of Whipsnade Tree Cathedral Fund.

D WHIPSNADE ZOO was originally known as Whipsnade Wild Animal Park. It's open from 10am every day except Christmas Day. You can drive round part of the zoo to view the Asian animals and there's a steam train on busy days in the summer.

E STUDHAM COMMON has been vital to the community for generations for livestock grazing and firewood. The Common's varied habitats support an impressively wide range of flora and fauna, including rare species such as the skylark, the hazel dormouse and several varieties of orchid. In 1997 The Friends of Studham Common were formed to help restore and replant hedgerows, reclaim lost grasslands and woodland glades, and reopen footpaths and bridleways. The Chiltern Society's Wendover Woods Conservation Group has been coming to Studham Common for several years, helping the Friends to restore hedges and creating wildlife habitats.

NEARBY CHILTERN SOCIETY WALKS
DUNSTABLE DOWNS AND KENSWORTH – Walk 1 of the *50 Great Walks in the Chilterns* book meets this route at the Tree Cathedral.

A Walk with Gordon & Dennis

WALK 6

The late Gordon Beningfield was an artist with an international reputation for his beautiful depictions of the natural world, both around his Hertfordshire home and further afield. He spent many happy hours wandering through the countryside with his close friend, naturalist and broadcaster Dennis Furnell. This walk in the Gade Valley is one of their favourites. The points of interest are described by Dennis.

Deep down, almost everyone has a need to know that they live in a world where the natural landscape and everything that belongs in it can flourish...
GORDON BENINGFIELD

LENGTH: 4 miles/6.5km
TERRAIN: An easy walk on good path surfaces and quiet lanes. Four climbs with a total ascent of 170m/560ft. One stile and a number of gates
START & FINISH: St John the Baptist Church, Pipers Hill, Great Gaddesden HP1 3BY. Grid ref: TL 029 112
FOOD & DRINK: The Alford Arms, Frithsden HP1 3DD

MAPS: OS Explorer 182, Chiltern Society 20
PARKING: Church Meadow, Great Gaddesden HP1 3BT. Grid ref: TL 029 112
LOCAL TRANSPORT: Bus 30 runs between Berkhamsted and Great Gaddesden, Monday to Friday. Bus 532 runs between Hemel Hempstead and Northchurch, stopping in Potten End, Monday to Saturday. Full details can be found on www.travelinesoutheast.org.uk

The Gade Valley

A Walk with Gordon & Dennis

River Gade water meadow

Kingfisher

ROUTE & POINTS OF INTEREST

From the lych gate entrance to the church, walk down the lane and bear right to the road T-junction. Turn right for a few metres and cross both the road and the stile opposite into a meadow. Follow the path to the river, and after walking beside it for 50m bear right up towards the right-hand corner of the meadow.

A **WATER MEADOW** The River Gade rises from springs further along the valley and creates a valuable year-round habitat. It's one of the few chalk streams suitable as a spawning 'redd' for rainbow trout. Our native species, the brown trout, also thrives here,. The quality of this mineral-rich water encourages large shoals of minnows and sticklebacks, food for kingfishers, grey herons and little egrets. It supports frogs and newts too, and a host of insects in summer, including the beautiful demoiselle; dragonflies include chaser, hawker and various migrant species. In the meadow the unsprayed grassland is alive with grasshoppers and crickets in summer, and the ever-changing flowering plants and grasses provide habitats for meadow brown, gatekeeper and ringlet butterflies, while marbled whites broadcast their eggs over the grasses that are their larval food plants. During June and July hawthorn hedges along the margin are a festival of bramble flowers, nectar for colourful red admirals, peacocks, comma, small tortoiseshell and sometimes the beautiful, fast-flying migrant painted lady butterfly – these beautiful insects were subjects for Gordon's superb paintings. In winter heavy rain can turn the meadow into a flood plain, supporting duck, grey wagtail and some waders. You might disturb a snipe feeding on water shrimps at the stream's edge.

Walk through into a field, follow its left-hand edge, pass a metal field gate and turn immediately right uphill towards the overhead cables. Go through the gate on the right, turn left and continue to climb up into a wood (High Park Wood).

B **HIGH PARK WOOD** Let your eyes rest on the gently folded land, the oaks and willows framing the sky, and the red kites. These elegant, fork-tailed birds seemingly float over the fields, searching for carrion and large insects. Primary scavengers, they will share territory, and it's not uncommon for several pairs to nest together. Buzzards, round-winged predatory birds of prey, need a large territory and drive out interlopers.

Ignore the path on the left and stay straight ahead to a path junction next to a deep pit. Turn left to stay inside the wood and walk along for 150m to the next junction. Turn left as the path descends to another junction

Peacock butterfly

and bear right out of the wood. Follow the path down the middle of the field to a road (Nettleden Road).

🅒 OPEN FIELDS BY NETTLEDEN ROAD
In late July, the ripening crops give the land a golden hue. Gordon wasn't a fan of monoculture, but he enjoyed the subtle colours against the green and lilac tones of the distant hill. Woodland was a favourite with Gordon and in spring these woods are rich with flowering ground cover like bluebells, primroses, yellow archangel, bramble and dog's mercury – indicators of ancient woodland. Hazel and hornbeam coppice stools show where felled trees grow new shoots. The poles were a source of natural materials for over 1,000 years for sheep hurdles and fence panels. Hornbeam charcoal was ground for gunpowder. Beech, ash, oak, yew and the late-lamented elm were used for furniture.

Cross Nettleden Road to the path opposite. Walk along the right-hand field edge to a path junction at the end. Turn left along the edge of the same field for 110m and follow the fence round to the right. Stay on this path as it climbs up between field and hedgerow.

🅓 HEDGEROW TOWARDS POTTEN END
The footpath is bordered by an ancient bank where badgers and foxes have dug setts and earths. The land has been grazed for many years, as can be seen from the presence of the anthills of yellow meadow ants. Gordon painted a green woodpecker investigating these anthills. In winter you might see migrant redwings and fieldfares. In spring and early summer the bank is a picture, with wild dog rose and the ground cover dominated by garlic mustard, so-called for its scent. It's the larval food plant of orange tip butterflies – look for the females whose wings are tipped with black; both sexes have a lacy pattern on the underwings, a little like lichen. She lays an individual yellow egg and when the caterpillar hatches it imitates the developing green pods. You should see these remarkably camouflaged larvae in June and July.

A Walk with Gordon & Dennis

Continue up past a disused gate and through the next one. After a few metres turn right, following the line of the overhead power cables, to a road. Walk along it and, where it bends up to the left, turn right directly downhill to a T-junction at the bottom. Turn right along the wide path.

E PATH FROM POTTEN END TO NETTLEDEN ROAD Twenty years ago you wouldn't have seen the silver-washed fritillary here. One of Gordon's favourites, he would be thrilled to know that they're flying around the honey-scented buddleia. In early spring the first butterfly is the brimstone, the butter-coloured-fly that gives its name to the worldwide butterfly family. It can be seen in every month of the year. The male's sulphur-coloured wings are quite startling. Brimstones hibernate in thick ivy in winter but come out when the sun is warm. Buckthorn is their sole larval food plant. It produces long straight twigs that were burned to make artists' charcoal. Blackthorn was used to make stock-proof hedges – a vegetable barbed wire! It also provides nest sites for migrant songbirds, like blackcaps, garden warblers, whitethroats and willow warblers, as well as being the larval food plant for the rare black hairstreak butterfly. In winter you may see a hunting sparrowhawk. In autumn we often looked at fungi. These fascinating organisms are neither plant nor animal, but have characteristics of both. Without their abilities as natural composters and recyclers our world would be uninhabitable.

At Nettleden Road, turn right and take the first left towards Frithsden and Ashridge House. Walk past The Alford Arms, turn immediately right down the lane and go straight on at the bottom. This is often referred to as the 'Roman Road' or 'Spooky Lane'. Climb up the steep hill past the vineyard to the top. There are now two options: stay straight ahead to drop down under 'The Devils Bridge' to a meet a road at the bottom, or turn left through a kissing gate into a field, then turn right downhill through two gates to the road.

F PATH TO ST. MARGARET'S This hedge is very old, with a rich mixture of native shrubs, one of which is the seemingly delicate spindleberry. It's becoming rare, because the spindles are no longer needed for spinning wheels. In winter it's decorated with bright, almost plastic-looking poisonous pink berries on greenish yellow twigs. Past The Alford Arms the fields have been managed sensitively, and barn owls hunt at dawn and dusk. The Romans once grew vines in the Gade Valley. Further up, a considerable growth of wild honeysuckle winds round the hazel. Honeysuckle is the larval food plant and hibernaculum for white admiral butterflies. Monoculture drove them out of this area in the 1950s – but perhaps with agriculture becoming less intensive this beautiful insect will return.

Stay on the path for nearly 1km until it reaches a road. Turn left along the road past the entrance to Amaravati Buddhist Monastery and turn right through a gate signposted to Great Gaddesden. Go through the next gate into a field and follow the path down through a further gate to the left of an electricity pole.

G PATH FROM ST. MARGARET'S TO GREAT GADDESDEN Where you descend to the churchyard, buddleia grows in the hedge and, when in flower, is full of the butterflies Gordon loved to paint. Churchyards themselves are peaceful places for wildlife and contemplation, and for listening to the winter song of wrens and robins.

Bear half-right down the field. Pass under the overhead cables to a gate in the bottom right-hand corner. Go through, follow the wall on the left for a few metres and go through a gate in the wall into the churchyard. Follow the path past the church and out through the lych gate to finish the walk.

Our special thanks go to Dennis and Ann Furnell for their enthusiastic support in producing this walk.

A Sense of Dacorum

WALK 7

This walk aims to demonstrate that modern Hemel Hempstead and its environs have much more to offer than cynics would have you believe.

> *Hempstead is a very pretty town, with beautiful environs.*
> — WILLIAM COBBETT 1822

The Water Gardens

LENGTH: 6.5 miles/10.5km

TERRAIN: Easy walking along urban pavements and country paths. Stile-free with a number of gates. One significant climb, and a total ascent of 130m/430ft

START & FINISH: Water Gardens car park, Bridge Street, Hemel Hempstead HP1 1EF. Grid ref: TL 053 069. Hemel Hempstead railway station can be used as an alternative start point

FOOD & DRINK: There are many places for refreshments in the town and on the walk including Fishery Wharf Café, Fishery Rd, Hemel Hempstead HP1 1NA

MAPS: OS Explorer 182, Chiltern Society 5 & 20

PARKING: Water Gardens car park – see above

LOCAL TRANSPORT: Hemel Hempstead bus interchange is located on Marlowes and Bridge Street. The town is also served by train services from London Euston. Full details can be found on www.travelinesoutheast.org.uk

Grand Union Canal

The old High Street

A Sense of Dacorum

THE ROUTE

From the car park make your way to the riverside and turn left along the path.

1 On reaching Combe Street turn right over the bridge, cross Waterhouse Street and continue ahead to the traffic lights. Cross at the pedestrian lights and turn left along Marlowes. Go over Midland Road and, at the next roundabout, turn right (signposted Old Town Centre).

2 Soon turn left up the High Street. Beyond the shops continue alongside the flint wall with Gadebridge Park on your left. At the roundabout cross the road and continue ahead through Piccotts End. Opposite No.152 (The Old Bakery) turn left onto the public footpath. Just after the footbridge, cross the busy road and turn right along the verge.

3 After 30 yards turn left past the entrance gate up the tarmac track. Go through the next gate into Homewood Park Farm, straight on past the farm buildings and through the gate directly ahead. Follow the grass track uphill. Continue ahead between fields and enter woodland. Keep to the main track across several path junctions, passing to the left of Halsey Field and to the right of some housing. Just after a row of garages go through the kissing gate and along the footpath with houses on your left and fields on your right.

4 On reaching the road turn right, cross over Parklands, and after 30 yards turn right onto the public footpath (signposted Potten End 1 1/2). Follow the path as it bends left round the edge of the field. Go through the kissing gate and ahead to the left of the hedgerow. At the driveway turn left to the road. Cross the road and pass through the kissing gate (signposted Chiltern Way and Grand Union Canal Circular Walk). Cross diagonally left to the far field corner with Boxted House to your right. Go through the kissing gate and continue ahead on the footpath.

5 At the lane turn right. Pass the pond and

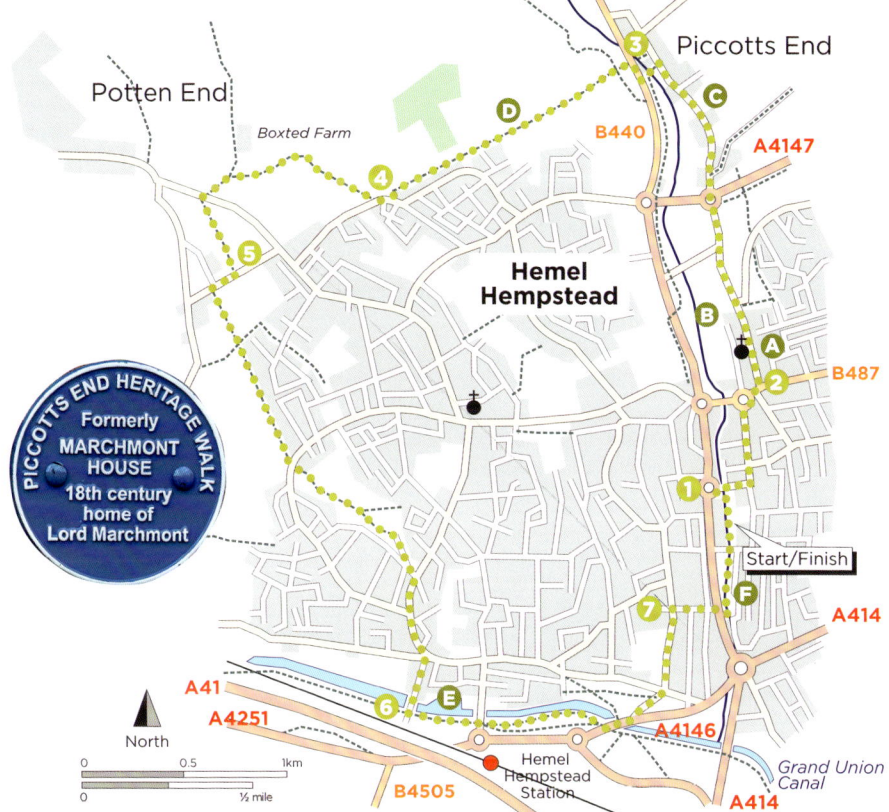

take the footpath on the left (Chiltern Way), soon passing to the right of a housing estate. On reaching the road (Long Chaulden), cross it and follow the footpath to the left of the adventure playground. Stay on the main track down to a small clearing with a path junction, and bear right along the enclosed footpath (signposted to Northridge). Soon reach an open space. Pass to the left of the children's playground, go straight across the grass, cross Shrubhill Road and continue ahead to the T-junction. At the T-junction (with mini roundabout) turn right and follow the road as it bends left. Turn right at the next mini roundabout into Chaulden Lane and immediately left down Old Fishery Lane.

6 Cross the canal bridge, descend the steps on the right and turn right along the towpath, passing under the bridge. (If returning to the railway station, take the steps on the right just before Bridge 149 and retrace your steps). Otherwise, continue until just before Grand Union Canal Bridge 150, climb the steps to the road and turn left. Take the next road on the left and walk up past The Church of St John the Evangelist. At the top of the slope cross the road. Turn right then immediately left along Heath Lane.

7 Opposite the school turn right down Charles Street. At the bottom, bear right to cross Cotterells, and go over the main road at the pedestrian lights. Turn right then immediately left along Moor End Road to reach the riverside. Turn left into The Water Gardens and walk along the river back to the car park.

OPTIONAL START FROM RAILWAY STATION

From the station entrance, walk down through the parking area to the main road. Cross at the pedestrian lights and go through the gate ahead onto Station Moor. Take the surfaced path across the moor and go through a gate to a road (Fishery Road). Cross, turn right along the pavement and take the first set of steps on the left down to the canal towpath. Turn right at the bottom to join the main route.

A Sense of Dacorum

POINTS OF INTEREST

HEMEL HEMPSTEAD NEW TOWN was one of the places designed to house Londoners made homeless by the Blitz and subsequent slum and bombsite clearance. Initial plans were drawn up by Geoffrey Jellicoe, whose vision was 'not a city in a garden, but a city in a park.' The first new residents moved in during 1949, and the town continued its planned expansion until the 1980s. Residential accommodation was divided into 'neighbourhoods', each with its own village centre. Much of the town's business and industry was located on the outskirts, particularly in the vicinity of the M1, which was built in 1959.

Piccotts End

A THE OLD TOWN'S HIGH STREET has been described as 'the prettiest street in Hertfordshire'. Our route passes historic buildings such as the Old Town Hall and St Mary's Church, artefacts such as the old plough and water pump near the car park entrance, and cobbled alleyways leading towards Gadebridge Park. Near the end of the High Street is Warwick House, winner of the Chilterns Building Design Awards, a collaborative venture between the Chiltern Society and the Chilterns Conservation Board.

B GADEBRIDGE PARK Roman remains were discovered, excavated and recorded in the area to the west of the Leighton Buzzard road, but have since been re-interred. The River Gade runs through the park, and has been undergoing improvements as part of the Revitalising Chalk Rivers scheme, with the aim of providing 'a continuous improved corridor for wildlife and people'. Here you'll also find the Forget-me-not memorial garden, designed as a reflective and attractive space for anyone who has been touched by the death of a baby.

C PICCOTTS END You enter the village past The Marchmont Arms, formerly a regency villa and the home of Lord Marchmont. There are a number of other Georgian and Regency villas, as well as some medieval cottages. A celebrated asset is the murals on the walls of one of the Grade I listed cottages (No.132). These images date back to the beginning of the 16th century and depict biblical scenes. Unfortunately they can only be viewed by the public once a year, during Heritage Open Days in September. On your right as you leave the village is the Grade II listed watermill, now converted into flats.

D HALSEY FIELD WILDLIFE HABITAT is a former school playing field, now cared for by members of Dacorum Environmental Forum and the Friends of Halsey Field, with help from other organisations including the Chiltern Society.

E THE GRAND UNION CANAL runs for 137 miles from London to Birmingham and was the main artery for goods between the Midlands and London for about 50 years. It's an amalgamation of several historic waterways. This section opened at the end of the 18th century as part the Grand Junction Canal, which linked the River Thames at Brentford to Braunston in Northamptonshire.

F THE RIVER GADE rises from a spring in the chalk at Dagnall, and flows through Hemel Hempstead, Kings Langley, then Cassiobury Park in Watford. After passing Croxley Green it joins the River Colne in Rickmansworth. It was once used to power watermills at Water End, Cassiobury Park and Two Waters, as well as the John Dickinson paper mills at Apsley and Croxley. It also supported the farming of watercress.

Ivinghoe Beacon & Ashridge

WALK 8

This walk follows the ancient Ridgeway with stunning views from the tops of both Pitstone Hill and Ivinghoe Beacon, before returning through the beautiful woodland of the National Trust's Ashridge Estate.

The Bridgewater Monument

LENGTH: 6 miles/9.7km, with a longer 8.7 mile/14km option

TERRAIN: A moderate stile-free walk on good surfaces which can be slippery at times. There are a number of kissing gates. The main walk has one steady and one steeper climb with a total ascent of 220m/720ft. The longer option has one steady and two steeper climbs with a total ascent of 330m/1,000ft.

START & FINISH: Tring Railway Station, Station Road, Tring HP23 5QR. Grid ref: SP 950 122
An alternative start point is the National Trust (NT) Ashridge Estate Visitor Centre car park.

Nearest postcode: HP4 1LT. Grid ref: SP 971 130

FOOD & DRINK: Brownlow Café at the Ashridge Visitor Centre and The Greyhound and The Valiant Trooper pubs in Aldbury

MAPS: OS Explorer 181, Chiltern Society 19

PARKING: Tring Railway Station or Ashridge Estate Visitor Centre – see above

LOCAL TRANSPORT: Buses 387, 389 & 397 run between Tring and Tring Station Mondays to Saturdays. The station is served by services from London Euston. Full details can be found on www.travelinesoutheast.org.uk

Ivinghoe Beacon & Ashridge

Ivinghoe Beacon from Pitstone Hill

THE ROUTE

This route follows The Ridgeway path to Waypoint 2. Leave the station, cross the road and turn right along the pavement. Cross over Northfield Road and stay in the same direction along the road edge for 100m to the entrance to Westland Farm. Turn left through the gate, walk up beside the concrete driveway and stay in this direction for 130m to a major path junction.

1 Turn left along the wide track for 550m and bear right uphill past the entrance to Aldbury Nowers Nature Reserve. Ignore the first path on the left, walk a few metres and climb the steps to the left. Follow the path through the woods for almost 1km before passing through a gate on to the grassy hillside of Pitstone Hill. Keep straight ahead, climbing round the side of the hill to the top and along the ridge, before descending to the car park. Cross the road and go through the gate opposite. Continue straight ahead, keeping to the left of the fence for 550m, to a path junction. *The optional longer route starts here.*

2 Turn right, follow the path uphill, go through a gate and on to a path junction at the top.

3 Turn right, go through a gate to the right of the kennels and stay on the wide track

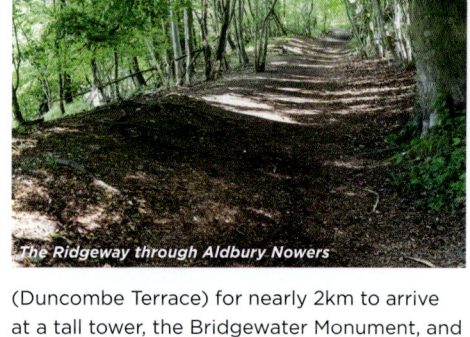

The Ridgeway through Aldbury Nowers

(Duncombe Terrace) for nearly 2km to arrive at a tall tower, the Bridgewater Monument, and the visitor centre.

4 Stay in same direction past them and take the wide path downhill. After about 200m fork right to continue to drop down to a road (Toms Hill Road).

5 Turn right and go over the road junction into Station Road. Walk past the pond, Post Office and village hall.

6 Just after the church turn right on a path signposted to Pitstone Hill. Go through two gates and left through a third just before a large barn. Follow the path through two more gates to reach a T-junction. Turn left and stay on this path to reach a road. Turn right to return to the station and finish the walk.

OPTIONAL LONGER ROUTE
This option continues to follow The Ridgeway to the top of Ivinghoe Beacon. Proceed in the same direction and climb the hill to the right of the dry valley (Incombe Hole). Ignore the gate on the right and continue on the stony track. Where that peters out stay straight ahead towards and through a small wood. Follow the path round the hillside, go through a gate and drop down to a road. Cross over and take the main path to the top of Ivinghoe Beacon. Continue along the ridge and go through the first gate.

7 Just before the second gate, turn right downhill. Go through the next gate near the bottom, continue ahead for 100m and turn right on a wide track across the middle of the field.

8 Pass through a gate, follow the path round to the left and go through the next gate into a wood (The Combe). Turn right through a conifer plantation and continue to a set of steps. Climb to the top and go through two gates into a farmyard.

9 Turn right, follow the waymarked route through the farm and leave on the concrete driveway. At the road, cross straight over, take a few paces into the wood and turn right. After 80m fork left and follow the path down to a major track (Duncombe Terrace). Turn left along the track to rejoin the main walk.

WALK 8

39

Ivinghoe Beacon & Ashridge

POINTS OF INTEREST

TRING STATION was opened by the London and Birmingham Railway in 1837 and was constructed by the railway engineer Robert Stephenson.

A THE RIDGEWAY NATIONAL TRAIL starts in the World Heritage Site of Avebury and crosses the chalk ridges of the North Wessex Downs and Chilterns AONBs – a total of 87 miles. The Chilterns section travels through woodlands, nature reserves and quiet valleys, also passing several magnificent viewpoints along the ridge. It follows a route used for at least 5,000 years by travellers, herdsmen and soldiers. Some people argue that it's Britain's oldest routeway, but this idea is generally out of favour today. For further information see www.nationaltrail.co.uk.

B ALDBURY NOWERS NATURE RESERVE is a Site of Special Scientific Interest (SSSI) managed by Herts and Middx Wildlife Trust. On the warm south-facing slopes there are many flower species typical of unimproved chalk grassland (milkwort, rock rose, clustered bellflower, lady's bedstraw) and possibly one of the rare butterfly species (Duke of Burgundy, green hairstreak, Essex, dingy and grizzled skippers).

C PITSTONE HILL is managed by the NT and is a nesting site for skylarks and meadow pipits. Directly below is one of the quarries of the former Pitstone Cement Works, which closed in the 1990s. This particular quarry is still producing chalk for agricultural use. The footpath runs alongside a section of Grim's Ditch. Named after a Nordic god, it's part of a series of linear earthworks that run from Bradenham to Ivinghoe, and remains one of the great mysteries of Buckinghamshire. Following investigations, archaeologists now generally agree that the earthwork probably dates from the early to mid-Iron Age, c700 BC.

D IVINGHOE The name comes from the Anglo-Saxon for 'Ifa's hill-spur'. In the Domesday Book it was recorded as Evinghehou. Some have claimed that Sir Walter Scott took the title of his novel *Ivanhoe* from the name of the village. The hills above the village are not only a SSSI, but also an area rich in ancient earthworks. Ivinghoe Beacon is one of the highest points in the Chilterns and has wonderful views. This important chalk grassland is home to a wide variety of butterflies and wild flowers. Incombe Hole is a steep-sided dry valley formed by glacial action.

E ASHRIDGE ESTATE Much of the area on this section of the walk is part of the Estate, which dates back over 700 years to when a monastery was founded. This continued to flourish until Henry VIII dissolved the monasteries in 1539. He bequeathed the Estate to the future Queen Elizabeth I, who lived there before being arrested by her half-sister Mary and taken to the Tower of London. Later, the Estate was bought by the Egerton family, one of whose descendants became the first Duke of Bridgewater. The most famous member of the family was the 'Canal Duke', who commissioned the building of the Bridgewater Canal. Opened in 1761, it's regarded as the first true canal in Britain. In 1853 the Estate passed to Lord Brownlow, whose family held it until 1925 when it was split up, with much of the parkland and surrounding area passing to the NT. The parkland is a haven for wildlife and is famous for its herds of fallow deer. The Bridgewater Monument was erected in 1832 in memory of the Duke of Bridgewater. It's 33m high with 170 steps to the top, and is open to the public.

F ALDBURY was listed in the Domesday Book as Elderberie, meaning 'old burh', or old fortification. The village has been used on many occasions by film companies. Notable productions include *Midsomer Murders, Inspector Morse, The Dirty Dozen* and *Bridget Jones*.

NEARBY CHILTERN SOCIETY WALKS

ASHRIDGE – Walk 18 of the *50 Great Walks in the Chilterns* book meets this route on Duncombe Terrace.

Dancersend Nature Reserve

WALK 9

Discover the treats that await you in and around the Reserve. In spring, look out for bluebells, primroses and cowslips; in summer, many species of butterflies and the Chiltern gentian; in autumn, fungi and the trees with their colourful display; and in winter the birds, which become a lot easier to spot.

Foxgloves in the Nature Reserve

LENGTH: 5 miles/8km

TERRAIN: A moderate stile-free walk on good surfaces, but can be muddy at times. Two steep climbs and a total ascent of 180m/590ft. There are numerous gates to pass through, including an unusual deer gate. Cattle are often grazing in the Reserve – they're essential for maintaining the grassland

START & FINISH: The café at Wendover Woods. Nearest postcode HP22 5NQ. Grid ref: SP 890 090. An alternative start point is the Dancersend Nature Reserve car park, Bottom Road, Tring HP23 6LB. Grid ref: SP 904 088

FOOD & DRINK: Wendover Woods café. None on route

MAPS: OS Explorer 181, Chiltern Society 18

PARKING: Wendover Woods pay & display car park

LOCAL TRANSPORT: None at the start. Bus 50 runs between Aylesbury and Wendover, Mondays to Fridays. On Sundays Bus 50 runs between Aylesbury and Ivinghoe and stops nearby on the B4009. Full details can be found on www.travelinesoutheast.org.uk

Dancersend Nature Reserve

The Reserve

Chiltern Summit, Wendover Woods

THE ROUTE

Facing the entrance to the new café, go left past the toilets and turn right following the Firecrest Trail. After 80m turn left on the Easy Access Hilltop Trail to a wooden barrier directly ahead. Do not go through, instead turn left uphill and follow this path through the trees to a bench on the right. Turn right immediately after the bench to meet the exit road for Wendover Woods. Turn right along it for a few metres to a footpath on the left.

❶ Take the path, bear round to the right by the electricity poles and follow the winding woodland path. Bear left at a fork, continue ahead, ignore the path to the left and go through a kissing gate into a field. Go straight across the middle and pass the next gate onto a road. Turn left along the road for 140m to a gate on the right signed for The Icknield Way.

❷ Go through the gate and continue along the bridleway, taking in the lovely views on the left towards Dancersend, Tring and Ivinghoe Beacon. Pass through a gate and stay on the main bridleway to a lane. Cross directly over into Pavis, Black and Northill Woods Nature Reserve and follow The Ridgeway for 500m to where a footpath crosses. Turn left onto the footpath and, after 100m, turn left down a sunken path to the bottom of the hill.

❸ Just before reaching a lane, turn sharp left on a bridleway for 300m to a 4-way path junction. Stay straight ahead on a footpath for a further 300m to reach a field gate. Go through into the yard of Dancers End pumping station. Turn right past the buildings, go through the brick gateway and bear right into the car park. *(Alternative start point).* Go through the gate on the right, walk through the meadow and bear left out of a gate into a lane.

❹ Cross directly over, through both the first gate and the second on the left, to enter Dancersend Nature Reserve. Follow the permissive path along the valley floor, bear left uphill through a gate and stay in the same direction as the line of overhead cables. The path then bends right under the cables and down to a gate. Go through, climb the steps ahead and walk along to meet a wide grassy track. Turn left

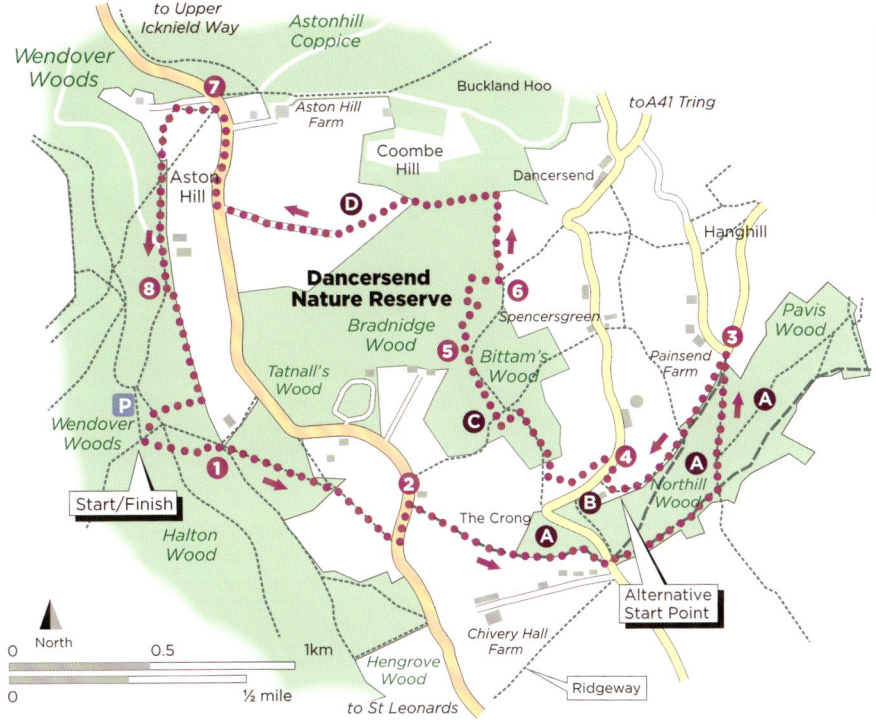

up the track, follow it round the right-hand bend, go over a crossing footpath and gently descend to a T-junction.

5 Turn right downhill for a few metres and fork left along a permissive path. Shortly after the path starts to descend, fork right, go through a gate and turn right to a bench dedicated to Susan Cowdy. From the bench, continue straight downhill to the bottom, passing an information board for the Duke of Burgundy butterfly. Ahead is another information board explaining the grassland management that takes place in the meadow behind. (If you have time, go through the gate on the left and explore the meadow). From the board go right along the fence line and through the right-hand gate ahead.

6 Cross the wide track and go past the board on the left for about 30m to where the Woodland Walk bears left. Continue straight ahead along the edge of the wood until the path ends. Turn left on a wide track along the valley floor, go through a metal gate and almost immediately bear right on a smaller path to pass through the next gate into a field. Bear half-left up the middle of the field, go under the overhead cables, and head towards a fence line and the large nesting box at the top. Pass through a gate, turn right and continue to climb to the left of the fence through three more gates to reach a road. Taking great care, turn right along it for 400m to a footpath on the left, just after the entrance to Aston Hill Lodge.

7 Follow this path for a few metres to a driveway, and turn right along it. Bear left at the gates to The Chalet, pass through a tall deer gate and continue to the main entrance road for Wendover Woods.

8 Turn left along it for 120m and, just before the right-hand bend, bear left on a path up into the woods. Turn right at the fence and follow the sometimes overgrown path along the edge of the wood to a cairn which marks the highest point in The Chilterns (267m/876ft). Take the wide path behind the cairn. Where it bends to the left, bear right and follow the path to the right of the access road to reach a gravel crossing path. Turn left over the access road to return to the car park.

Dancersend Nature Reserve

POINTS OF INTEREST

WENDOVER WOODS are owned by the Forestry Commission. Covering 325 hectares, they comprise a mixture of coniferous and broad-leaved trees. Once in the ownership of Alfred Rothschild, they were heavily felled during WWI to support the war effort. In 1919 the Air Ministry bought the site and planted conifers. Subsequently the Woods passed to the Forestry Commission, who planted beech, spruce, larch and pine. A Chiltern Society conservation volunteer group has worked with the Forestry Commission for many years to help manage the Woods for recreation, preserve ancient monuments and encourage biodiversity.

Pyramidal orchid

A BLACK, NORTHILL AND PAVIS WOODS
These ancient beech woods cover the steep slopes around the end of Dancersend Valley. They're owned by Bucks County Council, but managed by Berks, Bucks and Oxon Wildlife Trust (BBOWT). They have many interesting archaeological features, including old woodland and parish boundary banks, sunken trackways and deep pits where marl, a chalky type of clay, was dug to spread on the acid heath that could be found at the tops of these hills centuries ago.

B PUMPING STATION The Grade II listed structure was built by the Rothschilds in 1867, primarily to supply their estates at Tring, Halton, Aston Clinton and Waddesdon. In the early 20th century the site was taken over by Buckinghamshire Water Board, before passing to Thames Water Authority in 1975. An area of old chalk pits with a number of rare plants and insects is now managed by BBOWT as part of Dancersend Reserve, but access is by permit only.

C DANCERSEND NATURE RESERVE is a Site of Special Scientific Interest (SSSI) managed by BBOWT. Once part of the Rothschild family estate, the Reserve was established in 1939 in memory of Charles Rothschild, who set up the Society for the Promotion of Nature Reserves – regarded as the launch of the Wildlife Trust movement in Britain. The soil at Dancersend ranges from acid to alkaline, ensuring a wide variety of flora and fauna. There are ten types of orchid, including pyramidal, common spotted, bee, fly and greater butterfly. Other plants include Chiltern gentian, clustered bellflower, stinking hellebore and wood vetch. Look out for butterflies, including dingy skipper, green hairstreak and dark green and silver-washed fritillaries. Over 600 species of fungi have been recorded, including the remarkable collared earthstar, the outer layer of which splits and folds backwards into a star-shaped pattern. A signposted Tree Trail will introduce you to 12 species typically found in Chiltern woods. There's a memorial bench to Susan Cowdy who was a major figure in conservation both locally with the Wildlife Trust, and nationally with the British Trust for Ornithology and the Royal Society for the Protection of Birds.

D DANCERSEND RESERVE EXTENSION
The three fields, which were ploughed up for cereal production towards the end of WWII, were purchased in 1999 and are gradually being restored to flower-rich meadows. Some of the rarest plants on the Reserve have been established here, using seed collected by volunteers. Chalk scrapes have been excavated to create the right conditions for some of the most threatened butterfly species in the Chilterns.

This walk and the accompanying notes owe much to the assistance Mick Jones, warden for BBOWT at Dancersend. For further information go to www.bbowt.org.uk.

Cholesbury Hillfort, Grim's Ditch & The Ridgeway

WALK 10

The aim of this walk is to discover some of the prehistoric and historic features visible in this area. There's also an opportunity to look at some of the woodland archaeology of more modern times.

LENGTH: 6.8 miles/11km

TERRAIN: An easy walk on country paths and wide tracks. Numerous gates, nine stiles and 140m/460ft of ascent.

START & FINISH: The hardstanding area by Hawridge & Cholesbury Cricket Club, The Common, Cholesbury HP23 6ND. Grid ref: SP 932 071

FOOD & DRINK: None on the route, but The Full Moon pub is near the start

MAPS: OS Explorer 181 & Chiltern Society 8

PARKING: Hawridge & Cholesbury Cricket Club – see above (may be full at weekends during the cricket season); also in places along the edge of the common

LOCAL TRANSPORT: Buses 149 & 194 provide an occasional service between Chesham and Cholesbury/St Leonards on Tuesdays, Wednesdays, Thursdays and Saturdays. Full details can be found on www.travelinesoutheast.org.uk

Cholesbury Windmill

Cholesbury Hillfort, Grim's Ditch & The Ridgeway

Cholesbury Hillfort

THE ROUTE

From the parking area, turn right along the road and cross over the turning to Wigginton and Tring. Continue past the village hall and turn left on a path just before The Old Rectory.

1 Walk between the houses, go through the gate and follow the fence down to go through the gate at the bottom. Turn right through the next gate, and continue along the valley for 700m, ignoring paths to the left and right. Go over a stile into a field, bear left across the middle, then over three further stiles and through a gate to the next field. Bear left over this field and through a gate. Turn right along the lane, walk past the first entrance to Dundridge Manor and turn left into the second one. Walk along the driveway for 170m, and at the drawbridge on the left take the path directly opposite.

2 Go through the gate, follow the path across two fields and past two further gates to meet a concrete access road. Go through the gate directly opposite and stay in the same general direction across three fields and one playing field, over two stiles and through two gates to arrive at the main entrance to St Leonard's Church.

3 Continue to the road junction and go directly over the stile in the hedgerow ahead. Cross the field, go under the overhead cables and through a gate in the hedgerow. Bear right across the field for 70m to an unmarked path junction. Turn left to leave through a gate. Stay in the same direction across the next field and go through a gate into the grounds of Coppice Farm Park. Cross the car park and follow the access road to a lane. Cross straight over along Taylors Lane towards The Hale and, after 200m, take the path on the right just beyond Rowan House.

4 Follow the path through a wood, go over a stile and diagonally left across the field. Stay in this direction for 300m and look for a kissing gate to the left of the farm buildings.

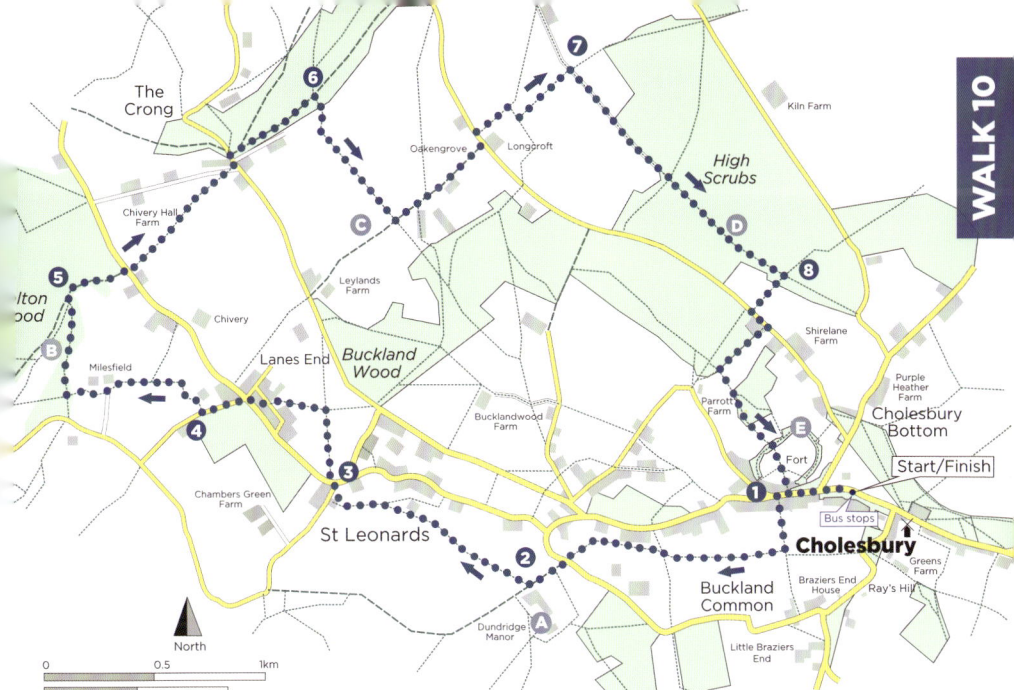

Go through it, and the one opposite, and follow the path between fence and hedgerow to a stile. Cross it, then after a few metres meet The Ridgeway and turn right along it. After 150m, where The Ridgeway descends to the left, continue ahead on a path through the trees.

5 Where the path rejoins The Ridgeway at a deep hollow way, turn right uphill and stay on this path to a lane. Cross it, go through the gate opposite and continue ahead keeping to the left of the hedgerow. After the next gate, bear left across the field, heading for a further gate between the mast and the farm buildings. Go through it to a road junction, then turn left past the mast and right into Pavis, Black and Northill Woods. Follow The Ridgeway for 500m to a major path junction.

6 Turn right into a field and walk straight across it to drop down the bank of Grim's Ditch onto a rough lane. Turn left along the lane and past a row of houses to a road junction. Turn left and, after a few metres, turn right past a barrier into a field. Follow the hedgerow on the right and where it ends turn right along the edge of a wood into a field. Turn left along its edge to meet a wide, rough track.

7 Turn right along the track for 600m to enter a wood (a wildlife conservation area). Ignore the first major path junction and continue ahead for a further 700m to the next junction. Turn right.

8 Go through the gate into a field and stay on the left-hand edge past the next gate into a lane. Turn left and, after a few paces, right on a narrow path. Walk along the path for 250m, turn left through a gate and stay on the field edge through two more gates into another wood. Keep straight ahead for 270m, passing through a gate, to arrive at the earthwork banks of Cholesbury Hillfort. After exploring the fort, return to the same point and go over the opposite bank to an information board and gate. Pass through it into a field and straight across to Holy (Holly) Pond. (Turn right to visit the church). Go through a gate to the left of the pond and straight ahead through two more gates to a road by the village hall. Turn left along the road to return to the start.

Cholesbury Hillfort, Grim's Ditch & The Ridgeway

St Leonard's church

POINTS OF INTEREST

CHOLESBURY & HAWRIDGE are two of four villages that make up the parish of Cholesbury-cum-St Leonards. The villages were established through gradual separation from Drayton Beauchamp and Marsworth-cum-Hawridge. The origin of the name Cholesbury is Anglo-Saxon, and it was mentioned in the Domesday Book.

A DUNDRIDGE MANOR is a Grade II listed house. The earliest records are from a charter c1187, granting the manor to Missenden Abbey. At the time of the Dissolution the manor passed to the Baldwin family until the house and lands had to be sold in lots. It was recorded as being in disrepair in 1769, but was later rebuilt. The original farmhouse has a number of 16th and 17th century alterations, and in the late 18th or early 19th century was encased in brickwork. One obvious feature is the ditch surrounding the house, which is believed to date from the 12th century.

B THE RIDGEWAY NATIONAL TRAIL
For more information see Walk 8.

C GRIM'S DITCH This major earthwork runs discontinuously from Bradenham to Berkhamstead/Potten End. It's believed to be late Iron Age, c100 BC. Its purpose is uncertain. It may have been a boundary of the Catuvellauni tribe's lands in the upper Chilterns, and/or a containment barrier for animals grazing in summer pastures. With an inner ditch and outer bank it's unlikely to have had any defensive purpose.

D HIGH SCRUBS Walking through these woods provides a wonderful opportunity to appreciate the relatively new science of Woodland Archaeology. The most obvious feature is the banks, which were constructed to mark boundaries and create enclosures. Others could include saw pits for cutting wood, charcoal hearths, or chalk pits where the mineral was extracted for building materials or fertiliser.

E CHOLESBURY CAMP AND THE CHURCH
The Camp is believed to date from the mid-Iron Age, and is some 2,500 years old. One of the most visually impressive prehistoric settlements in the Chilterns, it's oval shaped with a high surrounding bank and ditches, and covers about 10 acres. The first excavation in 1932 found evidence of a kiln and iron smelting. A geophysical survey in 2001 revealed evidence of other possible smelting sites. The fort interior is believed to contain a small deserted medieval settlement close to the church. Also within the camp is Holy or Holly Pond, reputed to have supplied good, clean water even in the most severe droughts. The church of St Lawrence was built in the 12th century and has an 18th century bell turret and roof. In the graveyard is a stone commemorating David Newton, a marine who fought at the Battle of Trafalgar.

This walk was created with the help of John Gover, an active member of The Chess Valley Archaeological and Historical Society and a keen walker. In 2001 he carried out a geophysical survey of Cholesbury Hillfort, which confirmed that the site had seen multiple occupations.

NEARBY CHILTERN SOCIETY WALKS
DANCERSEND NATURE RESERVE – Walk 9 of this book meets the route between Waypoints 5 and 6.
CHOLESBURY CAMP – Walk 15 of the *50 Great Walks in the Chilterns* book meets the route at the Hillfort.
CAPTAIN'S WOOD – Walk 25 of *50 Great Walks in the Chilterns* passes close by at Hawridge Court.

Following Two Different Ways

WALK 11

This walk follows two of the most important trails in the Chilterns, The Ridgeway and The Chiltern Way. There are stunning views, magnificent woodland and the opportunity to visit three of the Chiltern Society's most important sites – Lacey Green Windmill, Brush Hill and Whiteleaf Hill.

*Never came there to the Pink
Two such men as we, I think.
Never came there to the Lily
Two men quite so richly silly...*
RUPERT BROOKE

On Whiteleaf Hill

LENGTH: 7.2 miles/11.5km

TERRAIN: A moderate walk on easy but sometimes muddy tracks and along quiet lanes. Five stiles and numerous gates. One climb up to Loosley Hill, with a total ascent of 220m/720ft.

START & FINISH: Princes Risborough Library, Bell St, Princes Risborough HP27 0AA

FOOD & DRINK: The Whip Inn, Lacey Green and The Pink & Lily, Pink Road. Cafés and pubs in Princes Risborough.

MAPS: OS Explorer 181, Chiltern Society 3 & 7

PARKING: Horns Lane pay & display car park, Horns Lane, Princes Risborough HP27 0AW. The walk can also be started from the Chiltern Society's Whiteleaf Hill car park, Peters Lane, Monks Risborough HP27 0LH. Grid ref: SP 823 035

LOCAL TRANSPORT: There are various bus services to Princes Risborough, including Bus 300 which runs between High Wycombe and Aylesbury all week. Princes Risborough is also served by mainline trains to London Marylebone, the Midlands and Aylesbury. Full details can be found on www.travelinesoutheast.org.uk

Following Two Different Ways

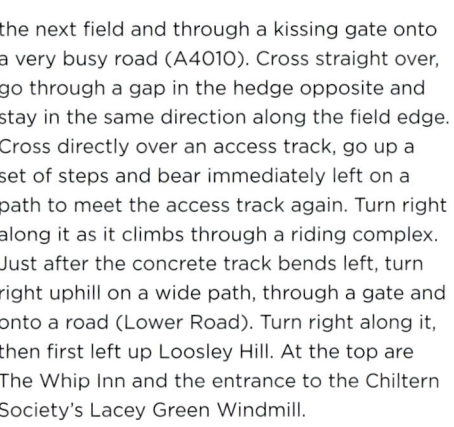
Princes Risborough from Brush Hill

THE ROUTE

From the library entrance turn right along Bell Street, go over Jasmine Crescent and continue to the pedestrian crossing just after Park Street.

1 Go over the crossing, turn left and immediately right up the surfaced footpath. Turn right straight after the metal barriers to emerge into a road. Turn left uphill, go over Merton Road and continue to a field at the end. Go straight across, drop down to a lane and turn right along it. After a few metres turn left over a stile into a field. Bear right down it and cross the next stile to a road (A4010).

2 Turn left, walk along the pavement for 600m and turn right along Upper Icknield Way. Cross over the junction with Shootacre Lane and continue uphill to Ridgeway Lodge on the left.

3 Just after the entrance, turn left on The Ridgeway across the middle of a field to a gate in the hedgerow ahead. Do not go through the gate but turn left to leave The Ridgeway and walk along the field edge following The Chiltern Way.

4 After 350m bear left across the corner of a field and over a ditch. Continue straight across the next field and through a kissing gate onto a very busy road (A4010). Cross straight over, go through a gap in the hedge opposite and stay in the same direction along the field edge. Cross directly over an access track, go up a set of steps and bear immediately left on a path to meet the access track again. Turn right along it as it climbs through a riding complex. Just after the concrete track bends left, turn right uphill on a wide path, through a gate and onto a road (Lower Road). Turn right along it, then first left up Loosley Hill. At the top are The Whip Inn and the entrance to the Chiltern Society's Lacey Green Windmill.

5 Cross Pink Road, turn right along the pavement and take the gate on the left just in

WALK 11

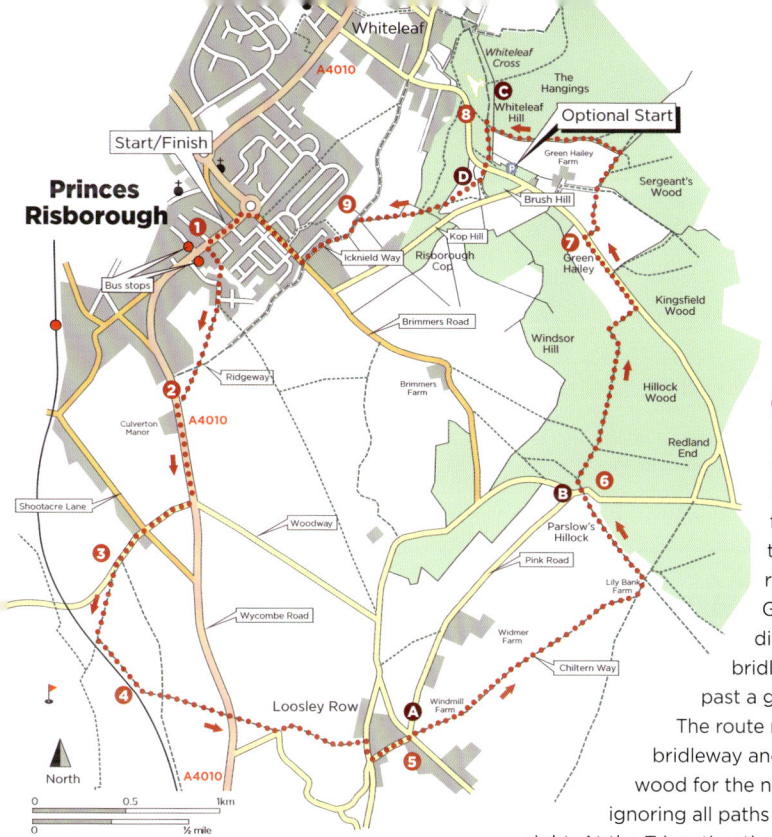

Princes Risborough

7 Go through the gate, bear half-left across the field and follow its edge to a gate in the right-hand corner. Go through, cross directly over a wide bridleway and go past a gate into a wood. The route now follows the bridleway and the edge of the wood for the next kilometre, ignoring all paths and tracks to the right. At the T-junction there is an option of a short diversion to the right to visit the top of the ancient Whiteleaf Cross.

8 Turn left past both the WWI trenches and the path up to Whiteleaf Hill car park. After 250m drop down to a lane. Turn right downhill for a few metres then take the slope on the left up to a gate. Go through it, turn left and stay on the path past the next gate. Bear right to admire the magnificent panorama from the stone toposcope at the top of Brush Hill. From there walk straight on to follow the path down the hill. Drop down a set of steps and through a kissing gate. Continue down the next set of steps, past an information board and out of the wood. Descend for another 300m to meet a T-junction and The Icknield Way.

9 Turn left along the rough lane to a road. Turn right and follow it downhill to a roundabout at the bottom. Turn left along Horns Lane and Bell Street to return to the library.

front of the bus shelter. Walk along the field edge, go through a kissing gate and stay in the same direction through two more gates into a large paddock. Bear right to cross a stile in the fence line. Turn left, follow the path between the paddocks for 300m and cross two stiles. Cross the field to the left of the electricity pylon aiming for a kissing gate in the middle of the hedgerow ahead. Go through and bear half-right to pass through a further gate at the edge of a wood. Turn left down to a lane then left along it for 550m to a road junction by The Pink & Lily pub. Turn right along the verge for a few metres and cross to a driveway past Woodlands.

6 Follow the driveway to the entrance to Hampden Lodge and take the bridleway to the right of it. Go through the gate and stay on the bridleway for 1km, ignoring all tracks left and right, to pass through a gate onto a lane. Turn left along it for 450m to a bridleway on the right just past Hailey Cottage.

51

Following Two Different Ways

POINTS OF INTEREST

THE RIDGEWAY NATIONAL TRAIL – for more information, see Walk 8.

THE CHILTERN WAY – for more information see Walk 1.

Lacey Green Windmill

A **LACEY GREEN WINDMILL** England's oldest remaining smock mill, so called due to its resemblance to an old-fashioned farmer's smock. The internal wooden machinery appears to date from c1650. During the 19th century it was rebuilt and modernised with fantail, patent sails, governor and machinery for grain cleaning and flour sifting, and continued working until 1915. In the 1920s it was used as a weekend cottage. Despite some attempts at weatherproofing, by the mid-1930s it was in poor condition. By the late 1960s the mill was in a desperate state, the whole body being twisted and tilted. In 1971 the Chiltern Society stepped in and volunteers, led by Christopher Wallis, began work to restore it. The project was completed in 1986 and in July 2013 it was given a prestigious Engineering Heritage Award by the Institution of Mechanical Engineers.

B **PINK & LILY PUB** Legend has it that the pub came into being in 1800 when Mr Pink, a butler from nearby Hampden House, and Miss Lillie, a chambermaid from the same house, fell in love and turned a private house into a hostelry. Rupert Brooke, one of the famous WWI poets, used to walk in the Chilterns and regularly visited the pub. He wrote a short, cheerful ditty about a particularly merry lunch there with his friend Jacques Raverat.

C **WHITELEAF HILL** In autumn 2014 the Chiltern Society took over the management of this nature reserve from Bucks County Council. The chalk hill figure of Whiteleaf Cross has dominated the local landscape for several centuries. Its full history is unknown but it's thought to have been constructed by the Saxon king Edward the Elder to commemorate a battle. The Bronze Age burial mounds date back to c3500-2500 BC. There are several WWI practice trenches at the southern end of the site adjacent to The Ridgeway.

D **BRUSH HILL** was transferred to the care of the Chiltern Society in 2013. It was designated a Local Wildlife Site in recognition of its importance as a haven for the wide variety of plants and animals that inhabit its chalk grassland, scrub and woodland. Depending on when you visit, you may be lucky enough to see roe deer, nuthatches and goldcrests, chalkhill blue butterflies, orchids, violet helleborines, bluebells, and even glow-worms.

NEARBY CHILTERN SOCIETY WALKS
HISTORY & WILDLIFE FROM GREAT HAMPDEN – Walk 12 of this book meets the route along the lane to The Pink & Lily.
LACEY GREEN – Walk 20 of the *50 Great Walks in the Chilterns* book meets this route at the junction of Lower Road and Loosley Hill.
BRUSH HILL AND WHITELEAF NATURE RESERVES – Walk 32 of *50 Great Walks in the Chilterns* meets this route just after Waypoint 7.

Whiteleaf Cross

History & Wildlife from Great Hampden

WALK 12

An interesting mix of history and wildlife in this peaceful part of the Chilterns. Add to that a couple of pubs, and what more could any walker want?

May the Lord level in the dust those who would deprive the people of their liberty.

JOHN HAMPDEN

Hampden House

LENGTH: 4.5 miles/7.3km
TERRAIN: An easy stile-free walk on good surfaces, but can be muddy at times. One short steep climb to the finish and a total ascent of 90m/300ft. There are a number of gates to pass through
START & FINISH: The Hampden Arms, Great Hampden HP16 9RQ. Grid ref: SU 845 015
FOOD & DRINK: The Hampden Arms and The Pink & Lily in Pink Road
MAPS: OS Explorer 181, Chiltern Society 7 & 12

PARKING: The Hampden Arms. The landlord has given permission to use the car park and would be delighted to offer you refreshments
LOCAL TRANSPORT: Bus 333 runs from High Wycombe, Tuesdays and Fridays. The Risborough Area Community Bus runs from Princes Risborough to Speen, Tuesdays and Saturdays. Full details can be found on www.travelinesoutheast.org.uk and www.racb.co.uk

History & Wildlife from Great Hampden

THE ROUTE

Turn left out of the pub car park for a few metres to the crossroads and turn right along the private lane directly opposite Memorial Road.

1 At the cottages, take the footpath to the right of No.21, walk along the edge of a wood and straight over the field ahead. Cross a farm lane and continue ahead through a gate into a field. Follow the fence on the left and go through a gate into the grounds of St Mary Magdalene Church. Take the path to the left of the church to a wide gravel driveway.

2 Turn left, walk past Turret House, go through the gate directly ahead and continue in the same direction on the wide grassy track. Go through a second gate and walk on for a few metres to a farm track at the edge of a large field. Turn right along the track and, where it turns to the right, continue straight ahead along the edge of the field. The earthwork on the right is Grim's Ditch. Where the track enters a wood, continue for a further 300m to a major path junction.

3 Turn left away from the disused stile, walk through a wood and along the field edge. Grim's Ditch is still to the right. Follow the path into a wood and stay in the same general direction for 270m to a path junction on The Chiltern Way. Bear slightly right to join this path and keep with it as it descends through a gate onto a road. Turn left and immediately right along a lane towards Lacey Green.

4 After 180m take the path on the right just after the entrance to a house called Pheasants. Go through the gate, bear left and follow the path through the wood. At a fork, bear left and continue for a further 400m, ignoring all tracks to the left and right, to a crossing bridleway. Turn left along it, go through a gate and left again on the driveway to a road. Turn right towards The Pink & Lily pub and turn left down Lily

Gorse

Bottom Lane. Follow the lane for 550m and take the path on the left just before Iron Beech Cottage.

5 Turn right immediately after the cottage and follow the path along the edge of a wood. This section of woodland is known as 'The Black Hedge'. Follow the path for 1km to a crossing bridleway.

6 Turn left along the bridleway into the wood. After 400m, cross straight over a wide forestry track and stay in the same general direction to drop down to a road junction. Turn right along Bryants Bottom Road and, after a few metres, turn left through a gate into a wood. Ignore the path on the right, go straight uphill on the main path and along to emerge at the edge of the cricket ground. Stay directly ahead past the cricket pitch to Memorial Road and turn left to return to the pub and the end of the walk.

St Mary Magdalene, Great Hampden

History & Wildlife from Great Hampden

POINTS OF INTEREST

GREAT HAMPDEN was mentioned in the Domesday Book as Hamdenam. It's the ancestral home of the Hampden family, the most famous of whom was the English Civil War hero John Hampden. A wealthy landowner and MP, he opposed King Charles I's imposition of Ship Money, a tax to raise funds for the Royal Navy. When the King tried but failed to arrest him and four other leading Parliamentarians in the House of Commons, it triggered a chain of events that led to the start of the Civil War. Hampden raised his own regiment and joined the war on the side of the Parliamentarians. He was mortally wounded at the battle of Chalgrove Field and later died at Thame. He was an important political and military leader, whose reputation was eclipsed by that of his younger cousin Oliver Cromwell. For further information visit the website of the John Hampden Society, www.johnhampden.org.

A **ST MARY MAGDALENE CHURCH** is situated a mile away from the main village and was built for the convenience of the Lord of the Manor. There has been a church on the site for many centuries. The current one dates back to at least the 13th century. John Hampden is buried somewhere under its flagstones. One theory is that his remains were hidden so that the Royalists couldn't desecrate them. In November 2017 the area round the church became the temporary home to a flock of hawfinches.

B **HAMPDEN HOUSE** There was probably a significant house on this site before the Norman Conquest. The land was held by a man called Baldwin on behalf of Archbishop Stigland. After the Conquest, it passed to William Fitz-Ansculfe and was held by Otbert. Reputedly, both Baldwin and Otbert were ancestors of the Hampden family. The current house dates from the 14th century and has been rebuilt and remodelled many times. The most significant changes took place after 1743, when the Gothic-style battlements were installed. In more recent times it was a girls' boarding school, and was subsequently bought by Hammer Films, who made many pictures there over a four year period. It then lay empty, but was eventually restored and is now used as offices, and as a venue for weddings and occasional filming.

C **GRIM'S DITCH** For more information see Walk 10.

D **PHEASANTS** was previously a pub of the same name, and was a regular haunt of the Hampden Estate's gamekeepers. John Tyler (see below) remembers an ex-poacher telling him that he once spent two hours standing motionless in the hedge opposite, with a brace of pheasant on his shoulder, when one of the gamekeepers' dogs spotted him through the window and sounded the alarm. Redland End was once a hamlet, consisting of a cottage, a pub and a chapel.

E **THE PINK & LILY** For more information see Walk 11.

F **IRONBEECH KILN,** now much altered, was originally a gamekeeper's cottage for the Hampden Estate.

G **MONKTON WOOD** The old, laid hornbeams along the SW edge of the Wood form a continuation of The Black Hedge, thought to be the oldest known parish boundary in Britain. It dates back well over 1,000 years and ran between Monks Risborough to the north and Princes Risborough to the south. Nowadays it's the boundary between Great Hampden and Lacey Green. The Wood itself is a fragment of ancient woodland and in medieval times was the main source of firewood for the people of Monks Risborough. With its mixture of beech, conifers, oak, birch and ash it's a good place to look for woodland fungi in the autumn. It's also home to birds such as nuthatch, great spotted woodpecker and, of course, pheasant.

This walk was created with the assistance of John Tyler, a keen naturalist and wildlife photographer – see www.johntyler.co.uk.

Bledlow & Lodge Hill

WALK 13

The walk starts from the lovely village of Bledlow which has been the setting for the TV series *Midsomer Murders*. From the top of Lodge Hill there are breathtaking views of the surrounding countryside and the eagle-eyed may even spot the Chiltern Society's windmill at Lacey Green.

LENGTH: 5 miles/8km

TERRAIN: Easy walking on good paths and along a couple of quiet lanes. There are four stiles, one of which is a little high and one that is bypassed, and a number of gates, as well as two climbs with a total ascent of 160m/525ft

START & FINISH: The Lions of Bledlow pub, Bledlow HP27 9PE. Grid ref: SP 776 019

FOOD & DRINK: The Lions of Bledlow. None on route

MAPS: OS Explorer 181, Chiltern Society 7 & 14

PARKING: If using the pub, you can park there, otherwise on the roadside around the village

LOCAL TRANSPORT: Bus service RCB Princes Risborough Circular runs Wednesdays and Fridays. Bus 320 runs between Princes Risborough and Chinnor Mondays to Fridays and stops on the nearby B4009. Full details can be found on www.travelinesoutheast.org.uk

View from Lodge Hill

Bledlow & Lodge Hill

South of The Lions of Bledlow

THE ROUTE

Turn left out of the pub car park and walk up the wide track. Where it bends to the right, continue straight ahead up the hill to meet The Ridgeway at a path junction at the top. The route follows The Ridgeway for the next 2.5 miles.

1 Turn left and, after 30m, turn right through a gate into a field. Bear left to follow the path across the field, then to the right of a hedgerow and fence. Just before the field ends, go through a gate on the left, turn right and continue along the edge of the field for 300m to reach a road.

2 Bear left across the road to go through a gate into a field. Cross straight over two fields to reach a further gate in the hedgerow ahead. Go through, turn immediately right and follow the path as it climbs gently uphill to the edge of a wood. Ignore the gate on the left and continue up the steep path to the top of Lodge Hill. Follow the path along the ridge enjoying the breathtaking views on either side. Go through a gate in woodland and continue ahead for 500m to a path junction. Ignore the stile on the right and bear left down the slope to the next gate. Go through, continue to descend to a field and follow its right-hand edge for 500m to a lane.

3 Cross straight over along the access road to Longwood Farm and take the wide track to the right of the farm gate. Follow the path between the fields to go through a gate, and after a few metres turn right. Follow the path between the golf club fairways to the next gate. Go through and, taking extreme care, cross the railway line to pass through a further gate to a path junction on the other side. Here the route leaves The Ridgeway and follows The Chiltern Way back to Bledlow village.

4 Turn left and stay on the path for 200m to reach a stile at the edge of a large house (The Old Rectory). Cross it, stay straight ahead and follow the driveway to a road. Go straight over through a gap in the hedgerow, stay in

The Lyde Garden

the same direction along the field edge and continue to the right of the hedgerow to cross a stile below the railway embankment. Climb the steps, cross the line with great care, drop down and go over the stile at the bottom. Follow the path for 200m and turn left through a gap in the hedgerow on a path which leads to the church of St Mary & St Nicholas, Saunderton. Go through the churchyard and out of the gate on the other side. Walk down the path and turn right along the lane. At the junction turn left along Bledlow Road, and after 50m turn right into Oddley Lane towards Chinnor and Bledlow.

5 At the left-hand bend, continue straight ahead through a kissing gate to the left of a private road. Follow the right-hand edge of the field and, where the fence ends, bear half-right across the field to pass a stile in the hedgerow. Turn right along the byway and, after 60m, turn left through a gap in the hedgerow into a field. Head directly across it to the left of a house with white chimneys. Go through the gate into a lane. Turn right along it, take the first left into Church End and continue past The Lyde Gardens and Holy Trinity Church to finish the walk at the pub.

Bledlow & Lodge Hill

POINTS OF INTEREST

Lodge Hill

BLEDLOW probably derives from the old English name of *Bledda* and secondly *hlaw*, meaning a hill or barrow. Holy Trinity Church was built mainly during the 12th and 13th centuries, and remains largely unaltered. The prominent tower houses eight bells.

THE LIONS OF BLEDLOW is a 16th century Grade II listed building and is formed from three shepherds' cottages. It's said that there were two pubs on the site, The Red Lion and The Blue Lion. The pub got its current name when the two amalgamated and is probably better known now as The Queens Arms in *Midsomer Murders*.

A THE RIDGEWAY NATIONAL TRAIL – For more information see Walk 8.

B LODGE HILL is a Site of Special Scientific Interest. Its ridge affords breathtaking views of the surrounding countryside. The site is mostly chalk grassland and scrub, and has been notable for such butterflies as Duke of Burgundy, grizzled and dingy skipper, brown argus, common blue, marbled white and hedge brown. There are also a few juniper trees, which used to dominate many years ago. There's also evidence of an early to mid-Iron Age settlement, as well as late Neolithic or early Bronze Age round barrows.

C THE RAILWAY LINE At this point the walk passes between the south and northbound lines of the Chiltern Railway. On the left is the northbound line which opened in 1862 as a single line branch from Maidenhead to Oxford. The southbound line, hidden in a tunnel and cutting on the right, opened just after 1900 to form part of the Great Western Railway's new service to Birmingham

D THE CHILTERN WAY – For more information see Walk 1.

E ST MARY & ST NICHOLAS CHURCH
Historically, Saunderton had two manors and two parish churches, St Nicholas and St Mary's. The former fell into disrepair and was demolished in 1452 with St Mary's being renamed as St Mary & St Nicholas. Built in 1227, it's Grade II listed. It had to be rebuilt in the late 19th century because the walls began to lean inwards. Wherever possible the original materials were used. The site of a Romano-British villa is located in the field just before the church.

F BLEDLOW MANOR & THE LYDE GARDEN
William the Conqueror granted the Manor of Bledlow to his half-brother Robert, who held it in 1086. The current house was build c1670 for James Blancks and was much extended in the early 18th century. In 1801 the Manor was sold to Lord Carrington and has stayed in the family ever since. The Lyde Garden is a small enclosed garden in a steep hollow valley – the source of the River Lyde – and has similarities to a rainforest. There's a high concentration of vegetation, including many moisture-loving plants like gunnera and hosta.

NEARBY CHILTERN SOCIETY WALKS

FOLLOWING TWO DIFFERENT WAYS – Walk 11 of this book passes very close to Waypoint 4 of the route.

Chorleywood to Chesham (Station to station)

WALK 14

Explore the hills and valleys of the Chilterns without the need for a car! The Chess Valley has some of the best countryside in the Area of Outstanding Natural Beauty, and is rich in wildlife. If that isn't enough, it's steeped in history!

LENGTH: 8 miles/13km

TERRAIN: A moderate stile-free walk on good surfaces which can be muddy at times. The route uses a few lanes, crosses a couple of busy roads and there are a number of gates to pass through. There are three climbs – total ascent 220m/720ft

START: Chorleywood Metropolitan Line Station, Station Approach, Chorleywood WD3 5ND

FINISH: Chesham Metropolitan Line Station, Station Approach, Chesham HP5 1DH

FOOD & DRINK: None on route, The Bedford Arms and The Red Lion are nearby in Chenies. Plenty of cafés and pubs in Chorleywood and Chesham

MAPS: OS Explorer 172 and 181, Chiltern Society 6, 17 & 28

PARKING: Chorleywood Metropolitan Line Station, Chorleywood Bottom, Chorleywood WD3 5JR

LOCAL TRANSPORT: Bus Service 103 runs between Watford and High Wycombe, Monday to Saturday. Full details can be found on www.travelinesoutheast.org.uk

Fishing on the River Chess

Chorleywood to Chesham
(Station to station)

The Chess Valley

Cottage in Chenies

THE ROUTE

From the station ticket hall exit turn left downhill, left under the railway and first right into Whitelands Avenue. Where the road turns left uphill, continue straight ahead. Soon after Carpenters Wood Drive, take the footpath on the left up into the woods, signposted for Barrel Arch.

1 Continue uphill past the information boards and, after a few metres, turn right on a wide path. Follow the path as it runs parallel to houses on the right, drops into a dip and then climbs to a path junction. Turn left and follow the path to the corner of the wood.

2 Turn right under the railway, Barrel Arch, and continue all the way to a main road, the very busy A404. Cross with care and walk along the lane into Chenies village. Turn left just after the school down to the Green. Turn left again up the gravel drive to the gates of Chenies Manor.

3 Turn right along the path between the walls of the Manor and the church down into a wood. Stay straight ahead as the path drops steeply to a road. Cross the road with care and bear right down the lane opposite. Turn left along the lane and over the River Chess to reach Mill Farm Barns.

4 Turn left and, where the gravel section ends, go left through the gate. Stay on this path for 1km to a gate on the right just before the road into Latimer village. Go through this gate and the next, cross the road, through the gate opposite and straight up the hill ahead. *The optional diversion to Neptune Falls starts here.*

5 Pass through the next gate, over the access road and take the path opposite past the front of Latimer Place. This section has the finest views of the whole walk. Go through the next gate, turn right uphill and follow the path round the top of the field. As the path starts to descend, look for a gap on the right. Go through, turn left and continue downhill to pass through another gate into a field. Stay straight ahead, keeping to the right of the hedge, through a series of gates all the way to Blackwell Hall Lane. Turn left down the lane.

WALK 14

6 Just before the left-hand bend, turn right along the gravel driveway to Blackwell Lodge. Go round to the left and through a gate into a field. Continue in the same direction through a series of gates to drop down to a bridleway. Turn left to a busy road and then right along the verge for 70m to a bridleway on the right.

7 Turn right through the gate, walk along the wide path and bear left up to and through a kissing gate. Follow the wide bridleway for 600m to a junction and bear left towards Botley. Stay on the bridleway for nearly 1km to a 4-way path junction.

8 Turn left and climb the hill ahead. At the top pass through a gap in the hedge into a field. Turn right along the edge for a few metres and bear diagonally left across the field towards the right-hand end of the hedgerow ahead. (The line of the path may vary depending on how it has been marked out after ploughing). Go through the wide gap into the next field, keeping to its right-hand edge. Go over the access road to Dungrove Farm, through a kissing gate and cross the field ahead.

9 On the other side pass through the right-hand gate, then turn left through the next one. Follow the right-hand field edge all the way to a pair of kissing gates at the far end. Go through the first and turn right through the second. Bear diagonally left across the field to a gate in the hedgerow. Go through it and follow the path downhill to cross the railway line. For the railway station turn right along the footpath, or to relax with some well-earned refreshments, continue ahead over the footpath and down a set of steps into Townfield at the bottom. Stay in the same direction over East Street, follow the pavement round to the right and reach Market Place and the High Street.

OPTIONAL DIVERSION TO NEPTUNE FALLS
After entering the field, bear left and follow the path to the next gate. Go through it and turn left to a bridge. Neptune Falls are on the right. To rejoin the main route, turn back towards the gate and follow the wide track uphill towards a lane. Near the top, turn left on the path that passes in front of Latimer Place.

63

Chorleywood to Chesham (Station to station)

Chenies Manor

POINTS OF INTEREST

A CARPENTERS WOOD is ancient woodland owned and managed by Three Rivers District Council. It mostly consists of beech, but there's also oak, cherry and hornbeam. In spring the woodland floor is a carpet of bluebells.

B CHENIES VILLAGE AND MANOR The village was first recorded in the 12th century when it was called Isenhampstead. It later became Isenhampstead Chenies from its connection with the Cheyne family, who built the Manor. It was shortened to Chenies in the 19th century. The manor house is a Grade I listed building which was visited by both Henry VIII and Queen Elizabeth I. For a time it was the seat of the Russell family (Earls, later Dukes of Bedford) before they decamped to Woburn. The gardens were voted Garden of the Year in 2009.

C DODDS MILL, originally Chenies Mill, was first mentioned as a corn mill in 1200. It later became used for fulling (where newly woven cloth was beaten and scoured with wooden hammers, stretched out to dry on tenterhooks and then combed). In the 18th century the mill was bought by the Dodd family who converted it to papermaking. In the 19th century it reverted to corn milling and later to production of cattle feed. It finally closed in 1933.

D THE RIVER CHESS is a chalk stream fed by groundwater stored in the aquifer – layers of chalk rock which work like a sponge, soaking up water until it emerges at ground level. Regular winter rainfall is needed to recharge the aquifer and keep the chalk streams of the Chilterns flowing throughout the year. Typical chalk streams like the Chess are shallow and narrow, with gravel beds and clear, warm water. We take our water from the aquifer too, so we need to use water wisely in order to reduce our impact on chalk streams and their wildlife.

E WILLIAM LIBERTY'S TOMB William Liberty, a local brick maker and relative of the founders of Liberty's of London, asked to be buried alone out of fear that he would not be able to identify his bones when the time came to be resurrected. Below the tomb is the site of the original village of Flaunden, where an information board explains its history.

F LATIMER VILLAGE is made up of a number of 17th and 18th century houses round a village green. Latimer House (now Place) was built in 1863 after the original Elizabethan house was destroyed by fire. Once the seat of the Cavendish family, during WWII the house became an interrogation centre for senior prisoners of war, including Rudolf Hess. It's now a conference centre and hotel.

G NEPTUNE FALLS The falls and the lake behind were formed in the 1750s by damming the River Chess. Until a few years ago there was a small statue of Neptune on top of the cascade. A mill once stood on this site, but was demolished in the mid to late 18th century.

H DUNGROVE FIELD This area was once owned and farmed by Thomas Harding, Chesham's religious martyr. He fought for the right to read the scriptures in English and in doing so became the last of the Lollards to die for his beliefs. The movement had been founded by John Wycliffe, an Oxford priest and academic, who attacked the power of the Roman Catholic Church over people's lives. These beliefs threatened the power and wealth of the Church, and in 1401 Henry IV enacted a statute requiring that Lollards who refused to recant their beliefs should be burnt at the stake.

NEARBY CHILTERN SOCIETY WALKS

THE CHESS VALLEY – Walk 29 of the *50 Great Walks in the Chilterns* book meets the route at Waypoint 4.

Metroland

WALK 15

This walk visits Rickmansworth and Croxley Green, whose current size and character owe much to the arrival of the Metropolitan Railway. The varied route includes woodland, fields, a moor designated as a Site of Special Scientific Interest, a village green, rivers and a canal.

> ... We called you Metro-Land.
> We laid our schemes
> Lured by the lush brochure,
> down byways beckoned,
> To build at last the cottage
> of our dreams,
> A City clerk turned countryman again,
> And linked to the Metropolis by train.
> — JOHN BETJEMAN

Rickmansworth Station

LENGTH: 6 miles/9.6km

TERRAIN: A stile-free walk walk on good surfaces with a couple of gates. The countryside sections can be muddy at times. One easy climb out of the valley and a total ascent of 90m/295ft

START & FINISH: Rickmansworth Station, Station Approach, Rickmansworth WD3 1QY. Grid ref: TQ 057 946. It's also possible to start the walk at The Green between Waypoints 5 and 6

FOOD & DRINK: Plenty of pubs and cafés in Rickmansworth, plus The Artichoke and Coach and Horses pubs on The Green in Croxley

MAPS: OS Explorer 172, Chiltern Society 28

PARKING: There are a number of car parks in Rickmansworth – see www.threerivers.gov.uk/egcl-page/car-parks. There is CitiPark opposite the station in Homestead Road and on The Green just before Waypoint 6 – WD3 3HX. Grid ref: TQ 069 957

LOCAL TRANSPORT: Rickmansworth is served by buses from Amersham, Hemel Hempstead, High Wycombe and Watford. Rickmansworth Station is on the Metropolitan Line from Aldgate via Baker Street and is also served by Chiltern Railways from London Marylebone. Full details can be found on www.travelinesoutheast.org.uk

Metroland

Canal near Rickmansworth

Almhouses, Rickmansworth

THE ROUTE

From Rickmansworth Station entrance turn right down the hill, right again under the railway bridge and walk down to the High Street. Go left along it for 90m and turn right past the bollards into Bury Lane.

1 Walk straight along to the left-hand bend and ahead through the entrance gates to The Bury. Follow the driveway to the house and bear left on a smaller path to enter the church grounds. Follow the path as it bears right, turn left through the wall, left again past the church, then right along the path through the churchyard. Just past the bollards cross the road, turn right along the pavement past the roundabout and, just before the pedestrian crossing, take the steps on the left down to the canal and Batchworth Lock Canal Centre.

2 Walk up the slope and over the bridge. Proceed along the canal bank for a 1km and take the steps on the left just before the first bridge over the canal. At the top turn right on The Ebury Way. Cross the bridge, follow the track under a railway bridge and continue until reaching a wide asphalt track coming in from the right opposite a metal gate.

3 Turn left onto Croxley Common Moor. Take the well-defined path straight across the Moor and go through a gate on the other side. Cross the bridges for both the River Gade and the Grand Union Canal.

4 After the canal bridge, do not turn right. Instead go straight ahead into a wood. Fork left, then right, then left up a set of steps. Continue straight ahead through an open area, past an information board and on along a narrower path. After 600m, fork right at a major path junction and bear left at the next fork.

5 Shortly turn left on a wide gravel track, soon crossing a railway bridge, and continue uphill. After a further 230m, turn right up a surfaced track through the wood (Public Bridleway 11). Go past a school and some houses to reach a road (Watford Road). Cross straight over and walk along the road to the right of the church. At the junction cross to the other side of the road and turn right along the wide verge, passing the war memorial and both The Artichoke and Coach & Horses pubs.

Croxley Common Moor

6 After a further 500m, just after a pair of benches, turn left on a wide path and follow the signs to the River Chess. Drop down a set of steps and up to a path junction. Fork right, walk along the left-hand field edge, up the slope and turn left.

7 At the bottom of the hill turn right along the path for 150m, then turn left. Cross the bridge over the River Chess and turn left along its bank for 400m to the entrance to a playing field.

8 Bear right just before the barrier and follow this path for 650m. Where the chain link fence on the right ends, turn right uphill past the entrance to Rickmansworth Park School and continue to climb up the surfaced path in the park. After 170m turn left across the grass towards the buildings. Cross the road bridge and turn immediately right down the steps. Turn left past the entrances to Waitrose and the station car park, walk down the hill and up the other side to finish at Rickmansworth Station.

Church Street, Rickmansworth

Metroland

POINTS OF INTEREST

'METROLAND' was a name coined by the Metropolitan Railway's marketing department to describe residential areas which were built to the northwest of London in the early 20th century. It promoted the dream of a modern home in beautiful countryside with a fast rail service to central London, and contributed to the rapid growth of both Rickmansworth and Croxley Green.

Rickmansworth was a manor given to the Abbey of St Albans when the latter was founded in 793 by King Offa. Cardinal Wolsey later held the Manor of le More in the valley in his capacity as Abbot of St Albans. The rivers Chess, Gade and Colne, which give the district its name 'Three Rivers', provided water for the watercress trade and power for corn milling, silk weaving, papermaking and brewing.

A THE GRAND UNION CANAL was the main artery for goods between London and Birmingham for about 50 years. The section through Rickmansworth was known as the Grand Junction Canal, and opened in 1805. For more information, see Walk 7.

B THE EBURY WAY follows the bed of the single-track railway constructed by Lord Ebury in the mid-19th century. It ran between Rickmansworth (Church Street) station and Watford Junction. Despite adding freight links to the canal and the paper mill in Croxley, it never paid its way and eventually closed in 1952.

C CROXLEY COMMON MOOR is a Site of Special Scientific Interest and Local Nature Reserve, consisting of 100 acres of historic grassland on the flood plain of the River Gade. There are more than 130 grassland plant species, and recently water voles have been recorded here. It also provides valuable habitat for invertebrates. On reaching the canal, note that the housing development to your right is on the site previously occupied by John Dickinson's paper mill (of 'Croxley Script' fame).

D CROXLEY HALL WOOD & THE GREAT BARN Our path through the wood (All Saints Lane) is believed by some to have been an ancient highway to the Manor of Croxley and the (later) adjacent Great Barn, which is just off the route. It's one of Hertfordshire's oldest timber-framed buildings, dating back to c1398, and is Grade II* listed. It can be visited either on special open days or group tours. (Website: www.croxleygreatbarn.co.uk).

E CROXLEY GREEN The first inhabitant to have his name recorded was Richard de Croxley, a Knight of St. Albans, in 1166. Two farms are listed in the 13th century, belonging to Ralph Pyrot and Simon Duraunt. Even today the names 'Parrotts' and 'Durrants' are familiar to local residents. Croxley's expansion was due in part to the arrival of the railway, but also, importantly, to the construction of the paper mill. The village green hosts the annual 'Revels', which featured in a 1970s TV documentary by John Betjeman.

F THE RIVER CHESS is a chalk stream that rises in the hills beyond Chesham and flows down to join the Colne at Rickmansworth. It once powered a number of mills. One of them was Scotsbridge Mill (just off our route between Croxley and Rickmansworth), which is now a restaurant. There were watercress beds (believed to have ceased operation in the 1960s) on the right just before our route crosses the river. For more information about the unique qualities of chalk streams, see walk 14.

G THE ROYAL MASONIC SCHOOL FOR GIRLS can be glimpsed on the hill to your right as you walk along the Chess. Having outgrown its Clapham site the school acquired Rickmansworth Park Estate, and the mansion was demolished to make way for the school buildings.

NEARBY CHILTERN SOCIETY WALKS
COLNE VALLEY WILDLIFE – Walk 16 begins at Rickmansworth Aquadrome, a short distance from Waypoint 2.

Colne Valley Wildlife

WALK 16

This walk gives you the chance to experience the abundance of wildlife found in many different types of habitat in the beautiful Colne Valley. It's a wonderful location for all ages to explore and enjoy.

Springwell Lake

LENGTH: 6.2 miles/10km, with a shorter option of 3.8 miles/6.1km

TERRAIN: A stile-free walk on good surfaces which can be muddy at times. There are a number of gates to pass through. One steep climb up through Old Park Wood, with a total ascent of 70m/230ft

START & FINISH: Café in the Park, Rickmansworth Aquadrome, Frogmoor Lane, Rickmansworth WD3 1NB. Grid ref: TQ 055 938. The walk can also be started from Rickmansworth Station, Station Approach, Rickmansworth WD3 1QY. Grid ref: TQ 057 946

FOOD & DRINK: Café in the Park and The Coy Carp pub, Coppermill Lane, Harefield UB9 6HZ

MAPS: OS Explorer 172, Chiltern Society 22 & 28

PARKING: Rickmansworth Aquadrome car park – see above

LOCAL TRANSPORT: Rickmansworth is served by buses from Amersham, Hemel Hempstead, High Wycombe and Watford. Rickmansworth Station is on the Metropolitan Line from Aldgate via Baker Street and is also served by Chiltern Railways from London Marylebone. Full details can be found on www.travelinesoutheast.org.uk

Colne Valley Wildlife

THE ROUTE

Take the wide, surfaced path to the right of the café and toilets, and walk alongside Bury Lake. Bear right, following the Batchworth Lake Circular Walk, to the next path junction and turn left.

1 Continue ahead, with the River Colne on the right and a wet woodland area on the left, for 650m to a path T-junction at Bury Lake. Turn right to the next junction.

2 Turn right and immediately left through a gate onto a rough path. Walk ahead for 80m to an open hide that overlooks Stocker's Lake. Return to the path, turn left and continue straight ahead through a gate to a wide grassy area. Follow the path through more gates, eventually reaching a path that runs beside the river. Turn left along it for 1km to reach a path junction at a footbridge.

3 Turn right to take the footbridge over the river on a path signposted towards Inns and Springwell Lakes. Follow the path around to the edge of Inns Lake to exit through a gate onto a lane. Cross to the car park opposite. Continue straight ahead through the car park, to go through a gate at the far end which is the entrance to Springwell Lake. Follow the path round the edge of the lake for 1.3km, passing Springwell Reedbeds on the right, to join a surfaced access road. Continue ahead for 200m and, just before the bridge, bear right through a gate onto the canal towpath. *Optional shorter route starts here.*

4 Turn right and follow the towpath for 1.6km to reach The Coy Carp pub in Coppermill Lane. Turn left along the lane, taking great care because the road is very narrow as it crosses the canal. Just after the left-hand bend, turn left into Summerhouse Lane and walk along it for 300m to the entrance to Hillingdon Narrowboats Association.

5 Opposite the entrance is a road signed for The Hillingdon Trail. Follow it up past the houses on the left for 300m, bear left through the metal barriers and continue uphill through Old Park Wood. (After 250m there's an option to turn right further into the Wood to see the woodland flora). Continue uphill on the main path and between fields to meet Hill End Road. Turn left along the road for 650m as it passes through the village of Hill End, until reaching a left-hand bend.

6 Bear right on a path past the entrance to Cripps Farm Bungalow. Go through a gate and follow the path ahead for 650m as it drops down by the side of a wood. Just before the next gate is a white metal post. It was one of about 280 erected in the 1860s to mark the points where taxes were due to the Corporation of London on coal being brought into the city. The post is Grade II listed. Go through the gate and continue downhill keeping the hedgerow to the left. Before the end of the field, bear half-right up to a gate and a farm track. Go through the gate and follow the farm track down to the entrance to Stocker's Farm. Don't enter the farm, instead bear right up the slope to pass through a gate into a field. Turn left and follow the field edge down to the next gate. Go through this and shortly reach a wide track. Turn left, follow it past some farm buildings then round to the right over the canal.

7 Continue straight ahead through a gate into the reserve. Follow the main path to meet a major junction. Turn right on a wide surfaced path back to the café.

OPTIONAL SHORTER ROUTE

Turn left and follow the towpath for 1.2km to reach Canal Bridge 175. Just before the bridge on the left is one of the Grade II listed white metal posts referred to in Waypoint 6. Go under the bridge and turn immediately left up the steps and over the metal rails. Turn right to rejoin the main route at Waypoint 7.

Colne Valley Wildlife

POINTS OF INTEREST

SEASONAL HIGHLIGHTS *Spring:* chiffchaff, Cetti's warbler, heron, little egret, swallow; *summer:* common tern, Daubenton's bat, purple loosestrife, southern hawker dragonfly, damselfly; *autumn:* great crested grebe, osprey, red admiral; *winter:* goldeneye, kingfisher, shoveler, siskin, redpoll, wigeon.

OTHER WILDLIFE *Flora:* spring wild flowers in the woodland could include dog's mercury, lords-and-ladies, wood anemone, wood sorrel, bluebells and the wonderful and nationally scarce coralroot bittercress. *Birds:* look out for gadwall, cormorant, occasional visits from smew, red-crested pochard, water rail, blackcap and black-headed gulls. Migration can bring many unexpected sightings. *Butterflies:* sunny days could bring out brimstone, orange tip, small tortoiseshell and peacock.

COLNE VALLEY PARK AND RICKMANSWORTH AQUADROME The Park covers over 40 square miles and extends from Rickmansworth in the north to Staines in the south. There are 200 miles of river and canal, and more than 60 lakes. It's very important for both wildlife and recreational activities. The Aquadrome is 41 hectares of open water, woodland and open space – one of six Local Nature Reserves owned and managed by Three Rivers District Council. Batchworth and Bury Lakes are former gravel pits that ceased operation in the 1920s. Gravel extracted from them was used in the construction of the old Wembley Stadium. Today the area is a haven for wildlife and is notable for its wet woodland.

A STOCKER'S LAKE, INNS LAKE AND SPRINGWELL LAKE are owned by Affinity Water and managed by Herts and Middlesex Wildlife Trust (HMWT). Stocker's Lake is particularly well known to birdwatchers, with common terns nesting on the floating rafts, and the largest heronry in the county.

Snake's head fritillary

B SPRINGWELL REEDBEDS are the largest in the London area. Look or listen out for birds like reed and sedge warblers.

C THE GRAND UNION CANAL – For more information see Walks 7 and 15.

D COPPERMILL LOCK This was the site of an old copper mill, built in 1803 by the Mines Royal Company. The copper was used for lining the bottom of Royal Navy ships and for the dome of St Paul's Cathedral.

E OLD PARK WOOD is a Site of Special Scientific Interest owned and managed by HMWT. It's varied woodland, mainly hazel coppice understory with standard oaks, and some large sweet chestnuts in the lower, more sandy areas. The Wood is noted for an abundance of flowers in spring, including bluebells, yellow archangel, lesser celandine, wood anemone and coralroot bittercress. Golden saxifrage and marsh marigolds grow on stream banks and around the pond. The pond is also important for dragonflies and amphibians. The Wood is rich in invertebrates and birds, including all three species of British woodpecker.

These notes were compiled with the assistance of Rob Hopkins, Reserves Officer, HMWT.

NEARBY CHILTERN SOCIETY WALKS
METROLAND – Walk 15 of this book starts from Rickmansworth Station.

West Wycombe & Hughenden

WALK 17

Chiltern hillwalking at its best, linking the National Trust (NT) estates of West Wycombe Park and Hughenden, with wonderful views over the surrounding area. Don't be put off by the amount of climbing involved, this walk is well worth the effort.

> *Like all great travellers, I have seen more than I remember, and remember more than I have seen.*
> BENJAMIN DISRAELI

LENGTH: 5.5 miles/8.9km

TERRAIN: A moderate to strenuous walk on good surfaces but can be muddy at times. Three significant climbs with a total ascent of 290m/950ft. There are a small number of gates, but the walk is stile-free

START & FINISH: Hellfire Caves car park, Chorley Road, West Wycombe HP14 3AP. Grid ref: SU 826 947

FOOD & DRINK: Pubs and cafés in West Wycombe, the Stableyard Café at Hughenden Manor and the Le De Spencers Arms just off the route on Downley Common

MAPS: OS Explorer 172, Chiltern Society 7 & 12

PARKING: Hellfire Caves car park – see above

LOCAL TRANSPORT: West Wycombe is served by many bus services from High Wycombe. The most frequent are service 40 to Thame, service 275 to Oxford and services 300/X30 and 321 to Aylesbury. Full details can be found on www.travelinesoutheast.org.uk

West Wycombe House

West Wycombe & Hughenden

Dashwood Mausoleum

Sunken path, west of Downley

THE ROUTE

From the car park entrance, cross the road and turn right down the pavement to the main road.

1 Turn left through the village and continue to the roundabout. Cross the road to the left of the petrol station into Cookshall Lane. Walk along the lane, go under the railway bridge and take the second path on the right just before the entrance to Cookshall Farm.

2 Follow the path uphill for over 500m to a junction and fork right at the steps. Stay on this path as it climbs up through the wood, cross over the next path junction near the top and continue to a road. Turn left past the school entrance, ignore the kissing gate to the left and take the wide path to the right of it. This path leads to a road junction with the High Street opposite.

3 Turn left down Plomer Green Lane, right at the bottom into Moor Lane and continue down to the gravel section and path junction. Fork right along the bridleway and go straight ahead past the NT sign for the Hughenden Estate. Leave the woods and follow the hedgerow on the right for 450m to the end of the field. Stay on the same track up through the woods to the buildings at the top. Ahead are the toilets and tearooms of Hughenden Manor.

4 Turn left along the top of the hill towards Naphill for 50m and bear left downhill to a wide track. Turn right and follow this track for over 500m to where the field on the left ends.

5 Turn left downhill towards Downley and, on reaching the bottom, continue directly ahead to climb out of the valley. Cross a major ditch, stay in same direction for a further 100m and bear right uphill. At the next path junction, ignore the gate on the right, cross the small ditch and continue ahead to the edge of open ground, Downley Common. Walk up the hill towards the left of the houses and fork left on a path through a gap in the hedgerow up to a playing field.

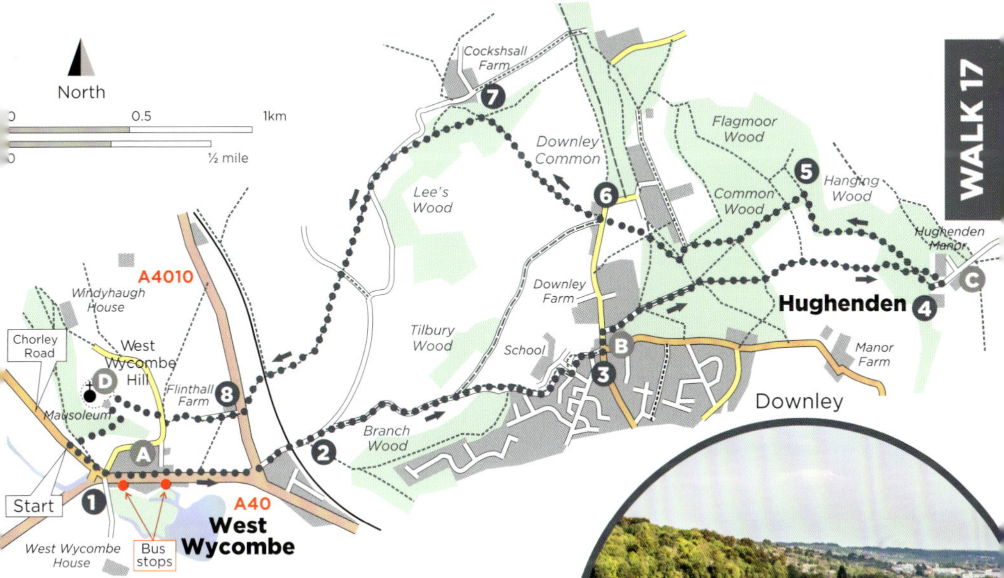

6 Cross it to a lane and take the path to the right of Downley Sports Pavilion. After a few metres turn left through a gate into a field. Follow the hedgerow on the right through the next gate and continue along the edge of the field for 400m to enter a wood to the left of the electricity poles. The path descends to a wide grassy track.

7 Turn left down to a lane and turn left along it. Just after the brow of the hill, bear right through a car park and ahead through a gap in the fence into a field. Head down the middle, go through a gap and cross the track to a path directly opposite. Climb up to a field and bear right along its edge. Where the track bends to the right, continue ahead along the edge of the same field. Go through a gap in the hedgerow, drop down under the railway line and bear diagonally left across the field to a busy road.

8 Cross it and go through the gate opposite. Keep to the right-hand side of the field for 170m and go through a gate on the right. Turn immediately left uphill to a lane, turn right along it for a few metres and take the path up West Wycombe Hill to the Dashwood Mausoleum, where you can admire the views and explore the buildings. Return to the front of the Mausoleum, drop down the slope towards High Wycombe and, after 50m, turn right onto a smaller path. Where the first set of steps ends, turn right down the remaining steps to a road and cross it to return to the car park.

View of West Wycombe

West Wycombe

West Wycombe & Hughenden

POINTS OF INTEREST

A **WEST WYCOMBE** Archaeological remains suggest that there may have been human activity in the area during the Mesolithic and Neolithic periods. The earliest known settlement was an Iron Age fort at the top of Church Lane. There's also evidence of Roman activity. The Dashwood family acquired the manor of West Wycombe in 1698. The house and grounds underwent complete transformation in the 18th century, carried out by Sir Francis Dashwood, 11th Baron le Despencer, and were passed to the NT in 1943. The entire village was sold by the Dashwood family to the Royal Society for the Encouragement of Arts, Manufactures and Commerce (Royal Society of Arts) in 1929. They carried out extensive repairs before handing it over to the NT in 1934. There are many 16th and 18th century buildings to be seen when walking through the village.

St Lawrence Church

B **DOWNLEY'S** name derives from the Old English word *lea*, meaning a clearing on the downs. It's formed from three hamlets, Downley, Littleworth and Plummer's Green. It has a long history of farming, as well as brick and furniture making. One of the highlights of the walk is passing through sections of Downley Common, which can be traced back to Anglo-Saxon times. Its more recent history can be seen in the number of banks or ditches used to mark boundaries, and the pits dug for clay, chalk or wood cutting. During WWII the Common was used to test Churchill tanks that were manufactured at the nearby Broome and Wade factory.

C **HUGHENDEN MANOR** was first recorded in 1086 when it was held by William, son of the Bishop of Bayeux. Its value was assessed at 10 hides. There have been various owners over the centuries, but in 1848 it was bought by Benjamin Disraeli, a future British Prime Minister, who felt that a country seat would help secure his political ambitions. He and his wife then started the task of remodelling the house and grounds. He died in 1881, leaving the estate to his nephew Coningsby Disraeli, who added the west wing in 1910. During WWII the house was used as a secret base for the production of target maps for bomber crews. The maps were developed from aerial photographs analysed at Danesfield House near Marlow. In 1947 the estate was passed to the NT, and in 1955 the house was designated a Grade I listed building.

D **WEST WYCOMBE HILL** is famous for several features: the Dashwood Mausoleum, St Lawrence Church and the Hellfire Caves. The Caves were excavated to provide both chalk for the new turnpike and work for the local population. They were later used by the notorious Hellfire Club. The Grade I listed St Lawrence Church stands on the site of an Iron Age fort. It was originally built to serve the lost village of Haveringdon, and was remodelled in its current form by Sir Francis Dashwood. Its crowning glory is the Golden Ball, which is large enough to hold six people and is reputed to have been a meeting place for the Hellfire Club. The design of the Mausoleum is based on the Constantine Arch in Rome. It was built to house the urns containing the ashes of the Dashwood family.

NEARBY CHILTERN SOCIETY WALKS

NAPHILL – Walk 31 of the *50 Great Walks in the Chilterns* book uses the same route between Waypoints 7 and 8.

CHILTERN RIDGES – Walk 33 of *50 Great Walks in the Chilterns* starts from the same car park.

High Wycombe & the River Wye

WALK 18

This is a chance to see not only where the Chiltern Society started out in 1965, but also to learn about the history of the River Wye and appreciate the work being carried out by the Revive the Wye Partnership.

Pann Mill

LENGTH: 5.5 miles/8.9km, with shorter 2.2 and 2.9 mile options

TERRAIN: An easy, stile-free walk along good paths and quiet roads, and using a number of pedestrian crossings. Some of the grass surfaces can be a little muddy after rain. No gates

START & FINISH: The Guildhall, High St, High Wycombe HP11 2AG

FOOD & DRINK: There are many places in the town. On the route there's Pizza Hut in Wycombe Retail Park, The General Havelock pub in Kingsmead Road and the café at the end of The Dyke

MAPS: OS Explorer 172, Chiltern Society 1 & 13

PARKING: There are a number of car parks fairly close to the Guildhall

LOCAL TRANSPORT: The bus station is next to the Eden Shopping Centre. High Wycombe is served by Chiltern Railways from London Marylebone. Full details can be found on www.travelinesoutheast.org.uk

High Wycombe & the River Wye

Waterfall, The Rye

Boats at The Rye

THE ROUTE

When facing the Chiltern Society plaque, take the archway on the right and walk down the pedestrianised street behind. Turn left along the right-hand side of St Mary Street, cross at the bend and walk down the steps to Queen Victoria Road. Cross it, and turn right then left through the paved gardens. Go over the pedestrian crossing and turn left to the information boards at the entrance to The Rye and Holywell Mead.

1 Follow the access road to the left, then continue straight ahead on the wide paved footpath to the historic Pann Mill and the River Wye. Stay in the same direction for a further 400m past a playground to a path junction. Cross straight over to join a gravel path and follow the stream to the left. The path first bends right then left, passing the bowls club. Walk along the Lido driveway to Bassetsbury Lane and turn right to the junction with Keep Hill Road. *The shorter 2.2 mile option starts here.*

2 After a further 60m, bear left along Bowden Lane towards a disused railway bridge. Go under this, and the large pipe, to view the pond on the right. *The shorter 2.9 mile option starts here.*

3 Continue in the same direction along the river bank, with the new Wye Dean development on the right. Cross the entrance road and, after 200m, follow the footpath round to the right to a roundabout in Wycombe Retail Park. Turn left along Ryemead Way and cross it via a traffic island by the river bridge. Continue straight ahead on the wooden walkway to the left of the Pizza Hut building and walk beside the river to a metal artwork. Turn left and take the pedestrian crossing over the main road. Turn right along the pavement past the Grade II listed St Anne's Church and Wycombe Marsh Baptist Church to a pedestrian crossing just before Gomm Road.

4 Cross the road, turn left for a few metres

High Wycombe

WALK 18

and right over the wooden footbridge into Kingsmead Recreation Ground. Turn immediately left and follow the riverbank path to the end of the playing fields, continuing ahead on a short section of The Chiltern Way. Cross the entrance to Kingsmead Business Park and follow the rough track to a T-junction. Turn right on the surfaced footpath for 130m to the next T-junction.

5 Turn right again along the bank of Marsh Brook (the Back Stream). Go past a car park on the right and stay in the same direction along the edge of the recreation ground for 630m. Bear left over a bridge just after the playground up to a road (Kingsmead Road). Turn right on the pavement for 100m and bear right down Beech Road to the ford at the bottom.

6 Do not cross it; instead take the surfaced path to the left and follow it back up to Kingsmead Road. Turn right along the pavement and stay on it to the road junction with Abbey Barn Road. Cross with care to continue along Kingsmead Road for 200m, and go over a footbridge into Bassetsbury Lane. Follow the lane for 600m through an S-bend, cross the bridge over the Back Stream and climb the grassy slope on the left to meet Keep Hill Road.

7 Cross the road, follow the stream to a waterfall and take the surfaced path behind it up to a path junction at the top.

8 Turn right along the wide path, keeping to the left of The Dyke, for 800m to reach the boating site and café at the end of the water. Bear right, follow the wide concrete path to reach the entrance to The Rye and turn left to retrace the route back to the Guildhall.

SHORTER OPTIONS

2.2 miles – Turn left up Keep Hill Road for 70m to the brick wall on the right. Turn right onto the grass and follow the stream as described from Waypoint 7.

2.9 miles – After the large pipe, climb the steps on the left to the disused railway line above. Turn left and walk along the old track to the end. Bear right down to Bassetsbury Lane. Turn right and follow the route between Waypoints 6 and 7.

High Wycombe & the River Wye

POINTS OF INTEREST

THE CHILTERN SOCIETY The plaque at the Guildhall was unveiled in 2015 to commemorate the inaugural meeting of the Society, which took place there in May 1965. The meeting was prompted by local protest over the proposal to cut the M40 route through the Chiltern escarpment. There was also a need to re-establish the Rights of Way network which had become overgrown and inaccessible during and after WWII.

THE RIVER WYE is a chalk stream, an internationally rare habitat which supports a wide variety of wildlife. (For more information about chalk streams, see Walk 14). It flows for 10.5 miles (17km) from West Wycombe through High Wycombe, Loudwater and Wooburn Green to its confluence with the Thames at Bourne End. The Revive the Wye Partnership was founded in 2007 to protect and improve the natural environment of the River Wye, its adjacent corridor, back streams and tributaries, for people to enjoy and wildlife to flourish. Other key aims are to improve public access to the river, to research and record its rich industrial and social heritage, and to make people of all ages more aware of its many attributes (www.revivethewye.org.uk).

A THE RYE AND HOLYWELL MEAD cover more than 53 acres. Rye Mead was used by local people for grazing cattle. Holywell Mead was the site of a Roman villa and watercress beds.

B PANN MILL The Wye has supported over 30 mills in its time. Although most have now disappeared, a notable exception is Pann Mill. There's evidence of mills on this site dating back to the 9th century. The current mill was restored after the main building was pulled down for road widening in 1971 (www.pannmill.org.uk).

C BASSETSBURY MANOR The Manor of Bassets Bury was granted by King John to Alan Basset in 1203 and comprised a manor house, a mill and a farm. It has an ancient tithe barn. The present building dates from c1746. Behind the bowls club is the still-intact Bassetsbury Mill, complete with water wheel.

D FUNGES MEADOW NATURE RESERVE is owned by Wycombe District Council and managed by Chiltern Rangers. It's home to many different species of flora and fauna.

E DISUSED RAILWAY The line was built during the 1850s and ran between High Wycombe and Maidenhead. The section to Bourne End was closed in 1970.

F WYE DENE has been developed on the site of an old sewage treatment works. Both the Wye and Marsh Brook flow through it and are a major feature. Look for the bubbling spring in the pooled area of Marsh Brook just on the right after the railway bridge. Sewage is now piped for processing at Little Marlow and the treated water returned into the Wye to augment its natural flow.

G WYCOMBE MARSH MILL once stood on what is now Wycombe Retail Park. The work of art represents the papermaking machines, and is engraved with the story of the Machine-breakers Riot of 1830.

H MARSH BROOK (the Back Stream) flows from the spring-fed watercourses in the grounds of Wycombe Abbey to join the main river in Boundary Park, Loudwater.

I THE DYKE is an artificial watercourse supplied by the spring-fed watercourses in the grounds of Wycombe Abbey and eventually becomes Marsh Brook. There are more details on the information boards.

This walk is based on a route devised by Roger Wilding, and the notes were compiled with the assistance of Mike Overall and Judy Sonley (all volunteers with the Revive the Wye Partnership), together with Jane Dunsterville of Flackwell Local Area History Group.

Christmas Common & Watlington Hill

WALK 19

This could be described as a Christmas walk for all seasons, or perhaps as a walk of two halves – a lovely woodland adventure or a breathtaking hilltop adventure. The choice is yours.

> *I loved the pitch and roll of the fields and their scatterings of chalk and flint, and the paths that dipped across them to sink into the darkness of the beech stands...*
>
> — IAN McEWAN

LENGTH: 5.3 miles/8.5km. For the figure of eight option both walks are 3 miles/5km, which could be shortened by parking nearer the pub

TERRAIN: A stile-free walk along good paths and some quiet lanes, with a number of gates to pass through. Care should be taken along the road from the car park. The main route has one long climb and one short, steep climb. Total ascent 200m/660ft

START & FINISH: Watlington Hill car park, Hill Rd, Watlington OX49 5HS. Grid ref: SU 710 935

FOOD & DRINK: The Fox & Hounds, Christmas Common OX49 5HL

MAPS: OS Explorer 171, Chiltern Society 9

PARKING: National Trust car park as above

LOCAL TRANSPORT: None at the start. The nearest bus services are in Watlington. Full details can be found on www.travelinesoutheast.org.uk

Christmas Common & Watlington Hill

Watlington Hill

View from Lower Dean Woods

THE ROUTE

Turn right out of the car park and walk to the road junction. Turn left towards Stokenchurch and, after 160m, turn right along a wide track towards Magpie Cottage.

1 Walk past the communications mast and, where the track bends right, continue straight ahead into the wood. Follow the path for 230m to a T-junction and turn right past the clay pits. After 100m fork left downhill and continue to descend for 800m to a path that bears right up the hill.

2 Take this path as it climbs steeply up the hillside. Near the top, bear left then right to continue climbing out of the wood. Walk between the fences and along a stony track between the houses to a road. Turn left along it for 100m through the village of Northend to a permissive bridleway on the right, almost immediately after the post box and shelter. The path can be a little obscured in the growing season.

3 Walk along the bridleway for 80m to a path junction, turn right and go through a gate onto a gravel driveway. Stay straight ahead on the driveway and, where it turns to the right, bear slightly left through the gate into a field. Walk along the left-hand edge of the field and stay in the same direction through four more gates into a wood. Follow the path through the wood for 350m to a path junction where the field on the right ends.

4 Continue straight ahead on the same wide path going gently uphill until it leaves the wood and meets a gravel track. On the left is the entrance to Queen and College Woods. Turn right along the track for 100m and turn left along a bridleway into a wood. Turn immediately right on The Oxfordshire Way and follow the path through the wood to a road. The Fox & Hounds pub is to the right.

5 Turn left along the road for 70m then right along the driveway towards The Tower.

Continue on the driveway for 80m to a car passing place, and bear right on a path into the wood. Follow the path for 330m to enter the National Trust's Lower Dean Woods and continue for a further 450m to near the edge of the wood. Follow the path round to the left. It opens out and offers lovely views over South Oxfordshire.

6 Enter another wood, turn immediately right and go through a gate into a field. Go straight on down the steep hill and through a gate at the bottom. Continue ahead to a junction of farm tracks and stay in the same direction for 500m to a path on the right just before the road. Turn right along the path, go through a pair of gates and climb up through a third gate.

7 Turn immediately left up a set of steps into the National Trust's Watlington Hill Estate. Follow the path along the edge of the wood and bear right up and onto the open hillside. Stay on the stony path until it peters out, continue ahead for 100m and bear right up the grassy slope to the top of the hill. Follow the track through a wide gap in the gorse and walk along the top of the ridge. Go past the wooden barrier and the posts in the ground to return to the car park and finish the walk.

FIGURE OF EIGHT OPTION

For the woodland adventure, follow the main route until Waypoint 5. Turn right past The Fox & Hounds and take the first left, signposted to Watlington, to return to the car park.

For the hilltop adventure, turn right out of the car park and walk to the road junction. Turn right at the junction and stay on the main road past The Fox & Hounds to join the walk at Waypoint 5.

Cottage south of Christmas Common

Christmas Common & Watlington Hill

Watlington Hill

POINTS OF INTEREST

CHRISTMAS COMMON There are many theories as to how the village got its name. They include a truce over Christmas between the warring parties during the English Civil War, an old local family name, or the abundance of holly trees. The communication mast close to Waypoint 1 is thought to be a US Air Force radio relay station which linked Daws Hill, High Wycombe to the base in Upper Heyford.

A NORTHEND is unusual in that the eastern half of the village is in Buckinghamshire and the western half in Oxfordshire.

B THE FOX & HOUNDS pub is Grade II listed and dates from the mid-18th century. It's constructed using both brick and flint, and the cottage at the back is timber-framed.

C THE CHURCH OF THE NATIVITY was built in 1889 as a chapel of ease for the use of those who couldn't get to the local parish church. It's now called Old Church and is a private house.

D LOWER DEAN WOODS are owned by the National Trust and have a wonderful display of bluebells in spring.

Approaching Watlington Hill

E WATLINGTON PARK is a country house and park. The house was built in the 1750s for John Tilson, son of the then Under-Secretary of State. Over the centuries the house has been subject to much modernisation.

F WATLINGTON HILL was donated to the National Trust by the Esher family, the owners of Watlington Park, in the 1940s. Most of it is part of a Site of Special Scientific Interest (SSSI) and is a nationally important wildlife site.

NEARBY CHILTERN SOCIETY WALKS
ASTON ROWANT – Walk 39 of the *50 Great Walks in the Chilterns* book is nearby.

Stanley Spencer's Cookham

WALK 20

Sir Stanley Spencer was one of the most important painters of the 20th century. This walk will take you round his home village, a place he regarded as 'heaven on earth'. It also ventures out into the surrounding countryside and alongside the Thames.

Cookham churchyard – Spencer's 'Angel'

LENGTH: 4.1 miles/6.6km

TERRAIN: An easy stile-free walk along pavements and country paths. One modest climb with a total ascent of 40m/30ft. A number of gates

START & FINISH: Stanley Spencer Gallery, High St, Cookham SL6 9SJ. Grid ref: SU 897 853. The walk can also be started from either Cookham Station, Station Hill, Cookham SL6 9BP or the National Trust car park, The Pound, Cookham Moor SL6 9SB. Grid ref: SU 892 853. Why not visit the gallery to find out more about this fascinating artist and his work?

FOOD & DRINK: There's a choice of pubs and cafés in Cookham, and on the route The Bounty Pub, Cock Marsh

MAPS: OS Explorer 172, Chiltern Society 32

PARKING: National Trust car park as above

LOCAL TRANSPORT: Bus 37 runs between High Wycombe and Maidenhead, Monday to Saturday. Cookham station is served by the Great Western Railway's Marlow branch line. It has direct trains to and from London Paddington during peak hours. Full details can be found on www.travelinesoutheast.org.uk

Stanley Spencer's Cookham

View towards Cookham Bridge

Path through Cock Marsh

BACKGROUND

COOKHAM The history of the area predates Roman times. It's thought that a Roman road from Silchester to St Albans crossed the Thames at a nearby bridge. Evidence also suggests there were Anglo-Saxon settlements. In the Middle Ages Cirencester Abbey owned most of the land. Development over subsequent centuries was limited by frequent flooding from the Thames. Expansion did take place over the higher ground around The Pound, and accelerated with the arrival of the railway in 1854.

STANLEY SPENCER was born in Cookham in June 1891 to William Spencer, a church organist and music teacher, and his wife Annie. He was home educated in a school run by his sisters Annie and Florence. He took art lessons at Maidenhead Technical College before entering the Slade School of Fine Art in London. At the outbreak of WWI he joined the Royal Army Medical Corps (RAMC), and his experiences had a lifelong effect on his work. After the war he was commissioned to paint an epic series of large-scale murals at the Sandham Memorial Chapel at Burghclere, but much of his art, including his religious works, featured the village life of Cookham. During WWII he was commissioned to paint scenes of shipbuilding near Glasgow. He was married twice, to Hilda Carline and later Patricia Preece, but his private life was very complicated. In 1959 he received a knighthood at Buckingham Palace, but died on 14th December the following year.

THE STANLEY SPENCER GALLERY Established in 1962, it's home to the world's largest collection of his works, and has an archive of letters, photographs, press cuttings and books. The building is a former Wesleyan Chapel built in 1846. Spencer attended the chapel with his mother, whose brother had been a local preacher there. In 2007 the Gallery was reopened, after renovation which created a modern, light space that displays Spencer's works to their best advantage.

THE ROUTE

From the Gallery, walk along the High Street past the Kings Arms to a house called Fernlea.

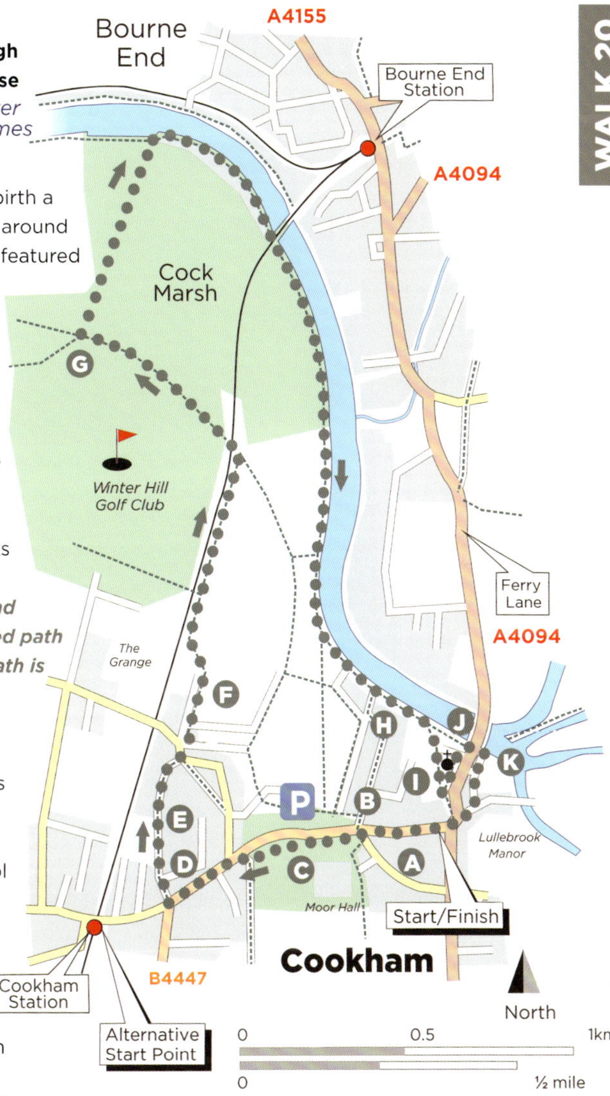

A **FERNLEA** Spencer's birthplace. Folklore says that at the time of his birth a crow fell down the chimney, flapped around and flew out the window. The house featured in a number of paintings including 'Neighbours – 1936' and 'Christ Carrying the Cross – 1920'.

Continue along the High Street as far as the War Memorial.

B **THE WAR MEMORIAL** carries the name of S Spencer MC. This was Sydney, Spencer's beloved elder brother, who died in the last few weeks of WWI.

Continue in the same direction and cross School Lane to join the surfaced path that runs parallel to the road. This path is known as The Causeway.

C **THE CAUSEWAY** Spencer would walk along this path every day on his way to the railway station and his journey to The Slade School of Fine Art in London, the premier art school in the country. He picked up the nickname 'Cookham' because of his love for the village, and his habit of coming home from London every day after classes. This walk is captured in the painting 'Cookham Moor – 1937'.

At the end of The Causeway continue straight ahead, walk past the mini roundabout and take the pedestrian crossing over the road. Turn left along the pavement to Belle Vue Cottages in The Pound.

D **THE POUND** The front gardens of these cottages were featured in the painting 'Gardens in the Pound - 1936'.

Walk along for a few metres and turn right into Poundfield Lane. The rough track climbs gently uphill and, just past a field gate, arrives at a large house on the right, Englefield.

View from Cookham Bridge

Stanley Spencer's Cookham

E ENGLEFIELD was built in the 18th century and is Grade II listed. Many of Spencer's paintings are associated with this property, including 'Cookham from Englefield – 1948' and 'Wisteria at Englefield – 1954'.

Continue up Poundfield Lane to a road junction. Turn left and immediately right on a rough track through a car park. Take in the view on the right towards the village, as well as Cliveden and Hedsor in the far distance.

F THE VIEW Just peeping through the trees on the horizon is the tower at Cliveden. On the hillside to the left is the beautiful hilltop church of St Nicholas, Hedsor. The Spencer family had strong connections to the church – Stanley's father, William, was its choir master and organist. When William was playing a loud piece of music, Stanley and his brother Gilbert would be required to blow the bellows. The view was also the scene for one of Spencer's more notable paintings, 'The Scarecrow – 1934'.

Continue in the same direction. Go through a barrier and along the edge of the golf course. Ignore the path on the left over the railway bridge and stay on the field edge down a set of steps to a path junction. Turn left through a gate, go under the railway bridge and bear immediately right through a kissing gate. Walk straight on, go through the next gate and follow the path round the bottom of Cockmarsh Hill. Turn right over a wooden walkway and continue straight ahead across Cock Marsh.

G COCKMARSH HILL While crossing the marsh, look at the hill behind. Spencer would walk to the top to capture the views. A particular painting of note was one of his second wife: 'Patricia at Cockmarsh Hill – 1935'.

Continue across the marsh and keep to the right of the mound to reach the bank of the Thames. Turn right along it and go through a kissing gate. Stay on the path past The Bounty pub, under the railway line and follow the riverbank for over 1km towards Cookham Reach Sailing Club. Go through two gates past the Club into Bellrope Meadow.

H BELLROPE MEADOW The name originates from the days when the area was used for the manufacture of rope.

Walk to the end of the meadow and bear right on the surfaced path into the grounds of Holy Trinity Church.

I THE CHURCH AND CHURCHYARD Holy Trinity is a 12th century, Grade II listed church with many later additions. It has some traces of Saxon masonry. In many of his paintings Spencer used both local people and landmarks as the backdrop to religious scenes. This is reflected in one of his most important works, 'The Resurrection, Cookham – 1924-26', in which he used neighbours and family members as models. On the right just past the end of the church is Spencer's memorial headstone, and at the end of the path by the gate is a statue of an angel. This became 'The Angel, Cookham Churchyard – c1936-37'.

At the gate, turn sharp left on an almost hidden path that runs between the boundary wall and the end of the church. Go through a gate and turn right to a gravel driveway. Turn left and take the path between River Gate and Stable Cottage to the riverbank by Ferry Cottage.

J COOKHAM BRIDGE Spencer spent a lot of time in and around the river, and this was reflected in his paintings, including 'View from Cookham Bridge – 1936'.

Turn right, go under Cookham Bridge and along the wooden walkway at the front of The Ferry pub.

K THE FERRY PUB was the scene of Spencer's famous painting 'Christ Preaching at Cookham Regatta – 1952-59', unfinished at his death and available to view in the Spencer Gallery.

At the end of the walkway turn right up Ferry Lane to its junction with Odney Lane. Turn right, cross the main road and turn left along the pavement to return to the Gallery and the end of the walk.

Our special thanks go to Ann Danks, Archivist at the Stanley Spencer Gallery, and Stephen Palmer, for their support in producing this walk.

Nettlebed Countryside Walk

WALK 21

This beautiful walk is centred on the historic Oxfordshire village of Nettlebed. It features two commons, a nature reserve and the wonderful Chiltern landscape of beech woodlands, chalk grassland and rich wildlife.

Brick kiln, Nettlebed

LENGTH: 5.2 miles/8.3km

TERRAIN: A moderate walk on good surfaces, but can be muddy. Two significant climbs with a total ascent of 190m/625ft. There are two sets of steep steps both up and down, numerous gates and a couple of stiles

START & FINISH: The Old Kiln, Nettlebed RG9 5BA. Grid ref: SU 701 868

FOOD & DRINK: The White Hart pub and the Field Kitchen café in Nettlebed and The Five Horseshoes pub in Maidensgrove

MAPS: OS Explorer 171, Chiltern Society 2

PARKING: The Green, Nettlebed RG9 5AX. Grid ref: SU 702 868

LOCAL TRANSPORT: Bus X38 runs between Oxford and Reading, Monday to Saturday. Full details can be found on www.travelinesoutheast.org.uk

Nettlebed Countryside Walk

Near Big Ashes Plantation

THE ROUTE

From The Old Kiln road, turn right towards the village and right again along Watlington Street.

1 After 130m turn right into Mill Road and walk up to the gates of the electricity substation. Take the path on the left and follow the white arrows for 380m to a wide track. Turn right along it and, at the houses, bear left to the end house.

2 Continue in the same direction between a wood and a fence for 300m to the driveway leading to Westwood Manor Farm. Cross straight over, bear right to follow a permissive path for 130m and turn right through a gate into a field. Turn immediately left past the paddocks and down through a gate at the bottom. Climb up the hill to the left of the fence and, where that goes right, continue straight across the field towards the house to the right of the farm buildings. Go through the gate and the one directly ahead. Follow the path past the end of a large barn, through the next gate and continue for 60m to drop down to a track.

3 Turn left and immediately right to reach a lane. Turn right and, at the grass triangle, turn right along a stony track past the entrance to Chears Farm. Follow the bridleway for 170m to a field gate.

4 Don't go through the gate, instead turn right over a stile into a field. Follow the left-hand field edge, stay in the same direction straight over the next field and go through a metal field gate. Turn left, follow the field edge and go over a stile into the next field. Follow the path downhill to the right of a deep pit and continue to descend to a gate in the bottom left-hand corner. Follow the path along the fence line and go through the next gate onto a bridleway. (Please note that the two stiles mentioned under this Waypoint are due to be replaced with gates.)

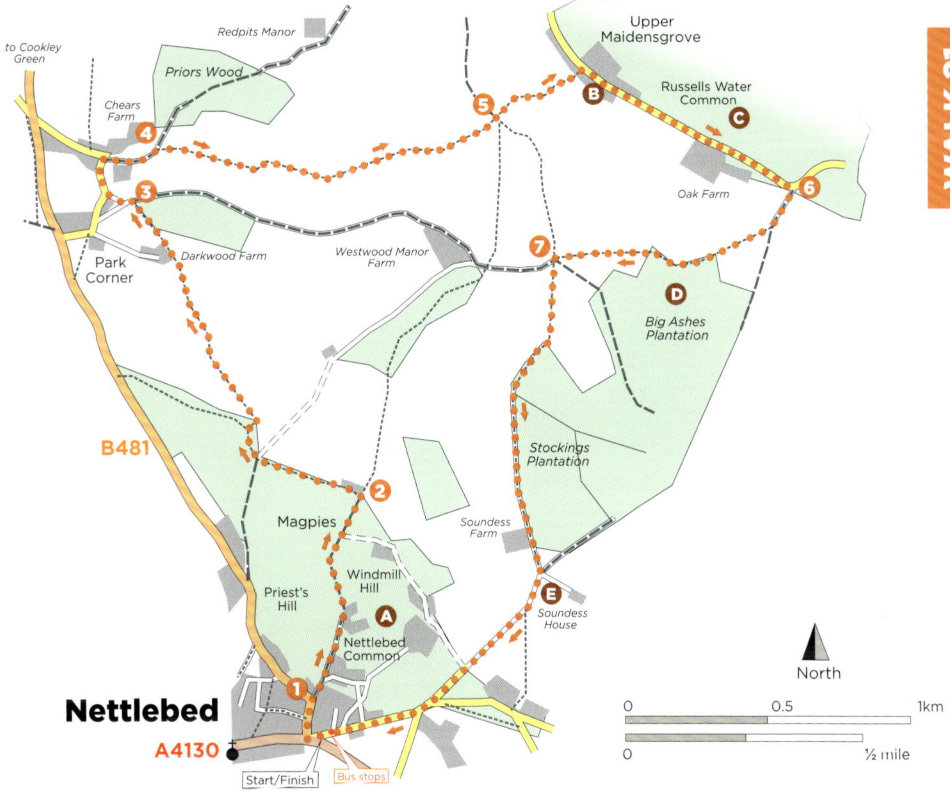

5 Turn left and immediately right through a gate. Climb up the steep slope, through a gate and up a set of steps. Continue along the path to a road. Turn right along it past The Five Horseshoes pub for 850m to the left-hand bend in the road.

6 Turn right, walk along a wide stony lane for 140m and fork right into a field. Drop down under the cables heading for a path just to the left of the corner of the woods, part of Warburg Nature Reserve. Follow the path along the top edge of the wood and through a gate into a field. Bear half-left down the field, through a gate and descend steep steps to pass through a gate into a field. Bear half-right down it and through a gate at the bottom to a path junction.

7 Go through the gate directly ahead and climb up under the cables towards the top left-hand corner. Go through a wooden kissing gate, follow the path at the edge of a beech wood and pass through the next kissing gate to the edge of a large arable field. Proceed along its edge. The path becomes a wide stony track, passing some cottages on the right. Continue to a junction by the gates to Soundess House. Turn right along the lane with fields on either side, and where it enters a wood continue ahead for 150m to a road junction. Turn right to return to Nettlebed and the end of the walk.

Sign at The Five Horseshoes

Nettlebed Countryside Walk

POINTS OF INTEREST

NETTLEBED Nobody is sure where the name originates, but there a couple of good theories. One is that Roman soldiers rubbed nettles on their limbs to keep warm on marches, and the other is that nettles were used in the production of sheets and table cloths. What Nettlebed was most famous for, however, was the manufacture of bricks, tiles and pottery. There was a plentiful supply of quality clay which allowed this industry to thrive from medieval times to the 20th century. At the starting point is the Grade II listed bottle kiln used for making bricks. Probably built in the late 17th century, it would have been one of a number in the area. It was converted in 1927 to burn lime. This ceased in 1938. It then fell into disrepair, but was restored in 1975. By the bus shelter are a pair of puddingstones and an information board.

Darkwood Farm, Park Corner

A NETTLEBED COMMON is one of a number that constitute the Nettlebed & District Commons. It provided many of the raw materials needed for the local brick making industry including clay, sand, water and firewood. The electricity substation is located on Windmill Hill. The mill that once stood here was burned down in 1912. The hill was also the site of a 16th century warning beacon.

B THE FIVE HORSESHOES is a 16th century pub with breathtaking views over the valley.

C MAIDENSGROVE AND RUSSELLS WATER COMMON Maidensgrove is in the modern parish of Pishill and Stonor. Its earlier names were Maiden's Grove and Minigrove. It's on the edge of the large area of common land known as Russells Water and Maidensgrove Common which belongs to Stonor Park.

D WARBURG NATURE RESERVE is one of the largest reserves owned by Bucks, Berks and Oxon Wildlife Trust. It has a visitor centre, picnic area, bird hides and a wealth of fauna and flora, including 15 species of orchid. It's home to an incredible variety of habitats sheltering thousands of species. In spring the woodland is awash with spectacular bluebells and wood anemones. In May and June the Reserve has a superb dawn chorus. When summer comes the wide, sunny rides and open glades of chalk grassland are full of summer flowers, including pyramidal orchids, as well as swathes of aromatic wild marjoram and thyme. During the autumn there are glorious colours throughout the tree canopy, while down below grow Chiltern gentians and an incredible 900 species of fungi. In winter, visitors can enjoy the magical frost along the valley bottom. See www.bbowt.org.uk/nature-reserves/warburg-nature-reserve.

E SOUNDESS HOUSE is an imposing manor house, changed and developed over hundreds of years, where it's reputed Nell Gwynne, mistress of Charles II, once stayed.

This walk was created with the help of Alan Futter, Chiltern Society Area Footpath Secretary in South Oxfordshire.

NEARBY CHILTERN SOCIETY WALKS
NUFFIELD & SWYNCOMBE – Walk 22 of this book passes close at Waypoint 3 – Park Corner.
WARBURG FIGURE OF EIGHT – Walk 45 of the *50 Great Walks in the Chilterns* book meets this route between Waypoints 5 and 7.
STONOR, BIX AND MIDDLE ASSENDEN – Walk 48 of the *50 Great Walks in the Chilterns* book passes close by at Lodge Farm, Maidensgrove.

Nuffield & Swyncombe

WALK 22

This walk follows The Ridgeway from the village of Nuffield over beautiful rolling countryside to the historic Norman church at Swyncombe. It returns to the start through woodland and open fields.

> *Never say 'no' to adventures. Always say 'yes', otherwise you'll lead a very dull life.*
> IAN FLEMING

LENGTH: 5.8 miles/9.4km

TERRAIN: A moderate walk on good paths and surfaces, with plenty of gates. Although stile-free, there's one awkward barrier at Waypoint 4. Two climbs, with a total ascent 150m/500ft

START & FINISH: Holy Trinity Church, Nuffield Hill, Nuffield RG9 5SN. Grid ref: SU 667 873

FOOD & DRINK: None on route except for the café at Nuffield Place, where walkers can get a free cup of tea after admission. The church offers tea and biscuits and has a toilet

MAPS: OS Explorer 171, Chiltern Society 2 & 10

PARKING: Holy Trinity Church car park. Please make a donation

LOCAL TRANSPORT: Bus X38 runs between Oxford and Reading, Monday to Saturday. The bus stops are by Waypoint 1. Full details can be found on www.travelinesoutheast.org.uk

Swyncombe House farm buildings

Nuffield & Swyncombe

St Botolph's Church

Park Wood

THE ROUTE

From the car park entrance, cross the lane and take the footpath opposite (The Ridgeway). The route now follows this National Trail as far as Swyncombe church. Cross the field, go through the gate and continue to the left of the buildings. Follow The Ridgeway marker posts across the fairways, taking great care to avoid flying golf balls. Just after the 4th tee turn right along a gravel driveway and left down a set of steps to the busy A4130 road.

1 Bear left across it and through the gate into a wood. Follow the path downhill and directly across the field ahead into a wood. Go straight over the junction with The Chiltern Way, cross and climb up the next field into a wood. Ignore a path on the left, continue through a metal field gate and pass Ewelme Park House to a crossing bridleway.

2 Go straight over onto a concrete drive, turn right behind the large barn and along a wide avenue to the edge of a field. Follow the right-hand edge, ignore the footpath on the right and, where the field edge swings sharply to the left, stay straight ahead into a wood. The path then descends steeply through a gate into a field. Continue downhill through the next gate onto a wide track. Turn right along the track for 500m and follow it round to the right to the entrance to Swyncombe church.

3 The route now leaves The Ridgeway and joins The Chiltern Way. Go through the entrance gate, take the path to the right of the church and walk along the avenue of yew trees to leave through a gate. Turn immediately left across the grass, fork left, cross the driveway and go through a gate into a large field. Follow the path uphill to the right of an enclosure and go through a gate into a wood. Turn immediately right to leave The Chiltern Way. Climb up through the wood, go straight over a path junction and continue for a further 150m to meet a surfaced driveway. Turn left along it, go through the gate at Swyncombe Lodge and stay in the same direction along the lane for 530m to meet a busy road (B481). Cross it and turn right along the verge to a lane. Directly opposite the lane there is a barrier in the hedgerow.

④ Recross the B481, go over the barrier into a field and turn immediately left along the edge into a wood. Turn right onto the bridleway and stay on it for 850m to a path junction where the fields on either side end.

⑤ Turn left, follow the edge of the wood to the houses and turn left into a field. Turn right along the field edge, walking beside the prison, to meet a path. Turn sharp left and, after a few metres, turn right on a permissive path into a wood (Park Wood). Continue ahead for 100m to a T-junction of paths.

⑥ Turn right along the woodland path, passing the grounds of Nuffield Place on the right, and go straight on to meet a road (A4130). Turn right, cross Bradley Road and walk along the pavement. Continue past the bus shelter and cross the road to the site of the old Crown pub. Turn right past the buildings and take the rough lane to the left of the A4130 up to Waypoint 1. The route now follows The Ridgeway back across the golf course to Nuffield church car park.

WALK 22

Nuffield & Swyncombe

POINTS OF INTEREST

NUFFIELD is a small village located at one of the highest points in the south Chilterns. There are two listed buildings in the village, Holy Trinity Church which dates from the 12th century, and the recently closed Crown pub. Just to the north is the A4130 Henley and Wallingford road which was a turnpike between 1736 and 1873. The village's best known resident was William Morris, the founder of Morris Motors, who later became Lord Nuffield. He was buried in Holy Trinity Church. The cemetery also contains the grave of broadcaster Sir David Frost.

Ⓐ HUNTERCOMBE GOLF CLUB opened in 1901, having been designed by Willie Park Junior, the owner of Huntercombe Manor. In 1926 it was bought by Lord Nuffield, who ran it until 1963. Ian Fleming, the James Bond author, was a member for 32 years until his death in 1964. It was the setting for the golf match between Bond and Goldfinger.

Ⓑ EWELME PARK was a deer park created in the 15th century by Thomas Chaucer, son of poet Geoffrey Chaucer. The original house was probably a hunting lodge. A brick house was built in the 17th century, and the current house dates from 1913.

Ⓒ ST BOTOLPH'S CHURCH & SWYNCOMBE HOUSE The name comes from the Old English words *swin*, for wild boar, and *cumb*, for valley or hollow. Every February the churchyard has a wonderful display of snowdrops and aconites. At this time visitors on a Sunday can usually enjoy homemade tea and cakes, and can also buy preserves and pickles. The church is named after the patron saint of travellers. It's of flint construction and was completed in 1020. It belonged to Bec Abbey in Normandy and was probably the poorest of the local parishes. Notable features are the oldest double aumbry (a cabinet for chalices) in England that is still in use; the 14th century

Ewelme Park

bell; the 17th and 18th century stained glass, and the restored medieval wall paintings. Swyncombe House was first established in the 13th century, but by the mid-16th century it was said to be in ruins. It was then rebuilt, but burned down in 1814. The current building dates from 1840.

Ⓓ PARK WOOD is owned by Nuffield College, Oxford and has a wonderful display of bluebells in the spring.

Ⓔ NUFFIELD PLACE AND HUNTERCOMBE HALL These are two major buildings located along Bradley Road. Nuffield Place was built in 1914 and bought by Lord Nuffield in 1933. After his death in 1963 the house was bequeathed to Nuffield College, who later gifted it to the National Trust. Huntercombe Hall was built in 1910. It was designed by Oswald Milne, a former assistant to the Arts & Crafts Movement architect, Edwin Lutyens.

This walk was created with the help of Steve Feigen and Stephen Fox of the Chiltern Society's South Chilterns Path Maintenance Volunteers.

NEARBY CHILTERN SOCIETY WALKS
NETTLEBED COUNTRYSIDE WALK – Walk 21 of this book passes close by at Waypoint 4, Park Corner.
SWYNCOMBE – Walk 43 of the *50 Great Walks in the Chilterns* book meets the route between Waypoints 2 and 3.
THE MAHARAJAH'S WELL – Walk 49 of *50 Great Walks in the Chilterns* also starts from Holy Trinity Church.

Checkendon Walk

WALK 23

This very pleasant walk explores the attractive woods and landscape in and around the village of Checkendon in South Oxfordshire. You can enjoy some refreshments on the way round at the award-winning Blue Tin Farm Shop.

LENGTH: 5.6 miles/9km
TERRAIN: A moderate stile-free walk on good surfaces, but can be muddy at times. One steep and one moderate climb, and a total ascent of 150m/500ft. There are numerous gates to pass through
START & FINISH: The Highwayman Inn, Exlade Street, Checkendon RG8 0UA. Grid ref: SU 659 818
FOOD & DRINK: The Highwayman Inn and Blue Tin Farm Shop

MAPS: OS Explorer 171, Chiltern Society 15 & 16
PARKING: The Highwayman Inn car park. The Inn opens at 9.30am to allow walkers to use the facilities. If you wish to have lunch or dinner there it's recommended that you book in advance – it's very popular
LOCAL TRANSPORT: Bus H1 runs between Crays Pond and Stoke Row on Thursdays. It connects to Bus H2 to and from Henley-on-Thames. Full details can be found on www.travelinesoutheast.org.uk

Red kites in flight

Checkendon Walk

Corker's Farm

THE ROUTE

From The Highwayman Inn car park turn left along the road for 40m to a footpath on the right immediately after Mulberry Cottage.

❶ Follow the footpath for 100m into a field and climb up its right-hand side. At the top, stay straight ahead to a path in the wood and turn left along it. Go through a gate into a field, and follow the fence to the left of the field for 390m to pass through the next gate into a wood.

❷ At the junction with a bridleway (Corkers Lane), turn left along it to a road. Turn left along the road for 100m, then turn right into a lane signposted to Hammonds Farm. Walk along the lane for 500m and, where it turns right towards the farm, stay straight ahead for a further 270m to a path junction at the entrance to a large field. Fork right along a restricted byway for 170m to enter a wood.

❸ Turn left past a barrier to join a permissive path through North Grove Wood. Follow the path for 450m and, just before a field gate, turn right downhill to join The Chiltern Way Extension at a T-junction. Turn right downhill to leave the wood through a gate into a field. Continue to descend, turn right through a kissing gate and walk between the fields to a lane. Turn right along the lane and, at the

The Chiltern Way above Bottom Farm

first right-hand bend, go left through a gate into the grounds of Bottom Farm House. Bear immediately left across the grass, to the right of the pond, and keep straight ahead to a path between a hedge and fence. Go through a gate into a field and follow the fence on the right. Where the fence bends to the right, stay in the same direction uphill to a gate in the hedgerow ahead. Go through the gate, climb up the steps to a path junction, turn left and continue uphill to a major path junction at the top.

❹ Turn right and immediately left to leave The Chiltern Way. Look to the left for wonderful views across the Oxfordshire Plain. Follow the path through the wood for 350m to a road. Turn right along it past Keepers Cottage and Blue Tin Farm Shop, and continue for a further 300m to the entrance to Garsons Farm on the left.

5 Just after the entrance turn right onto a path into a wood. After about 130m fork right steeply downhill and straight over a crossing path at the bottom. Follow the main track for 630m to leave the wood past a field gate and go along a rough access track to a lane. Turn right then immediately left, and follow the wide track round to the left. Go past a large barn on the right and stay on the main track to a cottage directly ahead. Pass to the right of the cottage for 100m to a metal field gate across the track.

6 Do not go through, instead take the gate on the right into a field. Go across the middle of the field, through a gate, and walk between the fences to a lane. Cross straight over to a path junction and continue past the tennis courts to the next junction and a pond. Turn right along the stony track, go round a left-hand bend and straight ahead through a gate into a paddock. Stay in the same direction to go through both a gap in the fence and a gate behind. Turn left along the narrow path and through the grounds of St Peter and St Paul Church to a road. Turn right along it, cross the lane to Hook End and, at the right-hand bend, turn left through a gate into a field.

7 Cross straight over the field, go through a gate in the hedgerow ahead and continue to a crossing path (Corkers Lane) at Waypoint 2. Go straight over, through the gate and along the right-hand side of the field. Go through the next gate, walk on for 50m, turn right down the left-hand side of the field and straight on along a path to a road. Turn left to return to The Highwayman and complete the walk.

The Highwayman Inn

Checkendon Walk

Langtree Cottage

POINTS OF INTEREST

THE HIGHWAYMAN INN dates back to the 16th century and was previously called The Greyhound. It's now described as a restaurant and café, and was the Chiltern Society's Pub of the Year for 2015.

EXLADE STREET Evidence of early man being in the area was found when a Neolithic flint tranchet axe dating from 3000 BC was discovered in the garden of Mulberry House near The Highwayman. Until the 18th century Exlade Street was a settlement of over 50 buildings, including 6 barns and several roadside ponds. It was a major stopping place one day's march from Oxford towards Reading. Musket balls have been found on the hillside, probably from a Civil War position. Several houses have remnants of a medieval cruck frame style of construction.

A NORTH GROVE WOOD is owned by the Woodland Trust. It covers 50 acres and is mostly mature beech with a scattering of ash, oak and cherry. It also contains evidence of quarrying and sawpits.

B BOTTOM HOUSE FARM GATE The gate up the hill from the farm was the first that the Chiltern Society's local team of volunteers helped to install. Since then they have installed over 300 gates.

C BLUE TIN PRODUCE is a small family-run free range farm in Ipsden, producing high quality rare breed meats using natural, traditional methods in a beautiful Oxfordshire setting. Their farm shop has a good range of locally sourced items, and has a great little café. In 2019 they were the South Chilterns area winner in the Chiltern Society's Food & Drink Awards.

D HORSE PATH The footpath from Scots Farm to The Black Horse is known as Horse Path. The Star Brush factory used to be at the edge of Stoke Row, and the horses working there came home alone along this path to their stable at the farm.

E CHECKENDON VILLAGE Records suggest there's been a continuous settlement in the area since the 7th century. The current population of 500 has remained constant since the national census in 1931. After WWII Checkendon hosted a camp for Polish war refugees displaced from the Middle East and Africa. It closed in the early 1960s. There are several noteworthy properties in the village. These include the Grade II listed Four Horseshoes pub (closed at the time of writing); Langtree Cottage which, although it appears older, is an elaborate Arts and Crafts house built in 1907; The Lodge (15th century); and Foundry House, part of which is a two-bay cruck beam house typical of the area, with a timber ring dating back to 1468. Opposite is the 12th century church of St Peter and St Paul, built by friars from the monastery at Bec in Normandy. The lych gate is the village war memorial, with names engraved along the top beams. The tower has eight bells, the earliest cast in 1765. Inside you can see dogtooth Norman arches and medieval paintings around the altar. There's also a Whistler window in memory of local artist and sculptor Eric Kennington.

This walk was created with the help of Alan Futter, Chiltern Society Area Footpath Secretary and Stephen Fox of the Chiltern Society's Path Maintenance Volunteers.

The history notes were written with the assistance of Tim Corbishley, a local resident and parish councillor.

Henley-on-Thames – Town, River & Woodland

WALK 24

This walk is packed with so much of interest it's impossible to describe it all here. It includes the history and architecture of Henley, the picturesque Thames and the natural beauty of Chiltern woodland.

River Thames at Henley

LENGTH: 11.5 miles/18.5km

TERRAIN: Although quite a long route, it's fairly easy stile-free walking along good paths, quiet lanes and urban pavements. There are two steady climbs with a total ascent of 220m/720ft, numerous gates and one low barrier

START & FINISH: The Town Hall, Market Place, Henley-on-Thames RG9 2AQ

FOOD & DRINK: There are many places in the town. On the route there's The Bottle & Glass Inn in Binfield Heath, and Greys Court for National Trust (NT) members

MAPS: OS Explorer 171, Chiltern Society 2, 4 & 31

PARKING: Several car parks fairly close to the Town Hall

LOCAL TRANSPORT: There are bus services to Henley from High Wycombe, Marlow, Oxford and Reading. Henley station is served by the Great Western Railway's Twyford branch line. Full details can be found on www.travelinesoutheast.org.uk

Henley-on-Thames – Town, River & Woodland

Henley Market

THE ROUTE

From the Town Hall, walk straight along Market Place and Hart Street to a road junction between St Mary's Church and the river bridge.

1 Turn right along Thameside, cross the road to the riverbank and turn right along it. The route now follows The Thames Path for 1.5 miles as far as Poplar Eyot Court in Lower Shiplake. Continue along the riverbank, pausing to read the information boards on the way. Just after The Old House, turn left and take the wooden walkway over Marsh Lock. Continue along the bank and follow the river round to the right. Go over a wooden bridge and past Thameside Court, which has a Swiss style narrow-gauge railway built by the current owner. Stay straight ahead along the surfaced lane to a junction just after Poplar Eyot Court.

2 Turn right along the unsurfaced lane. The route now follows The Chiltern Way to just past Greys Court. Cross over the railway line and proceed along the wide avenue to meet the very busy A4155 road. Cross to the wide byway opposite and stay on it for over 700m as it climbs steadily to a road junction near the entrance to Cray House. Cross straight over to the private road opposite and follow it to the end at the entrance to Highwood House.

3 Go past the entrance to the house into High Wood and, after 50m, fork right. Stay on the main path through the wood for 600m and go past a gate to a road (Harpsden Road). Turn left along it to a gravel driveway on the right on the outskirts of Binfield Heath.

4 Turn right past the front of The Bottle & Glass Inn and some farm buildings onto a narrower track (Bones Lane). The path follows the field round to the right to a path junction at the edge of a wood. Fork left and stay on the main path for 1.25km through Crowsley Park Wood to a lane. Turn left along it for 100m to a turning on the right.

5 Turn right into the lane and follow it, still on The Chiltern Way, as it climbs gently up to The Old Barn. Continue past the entrance as the lane becomes unsurfaced and stay on the main track for 1.3km to a path junction just after Cross Lanes Farm. Go straight over and through a gate. Follow the track for 1.2km and

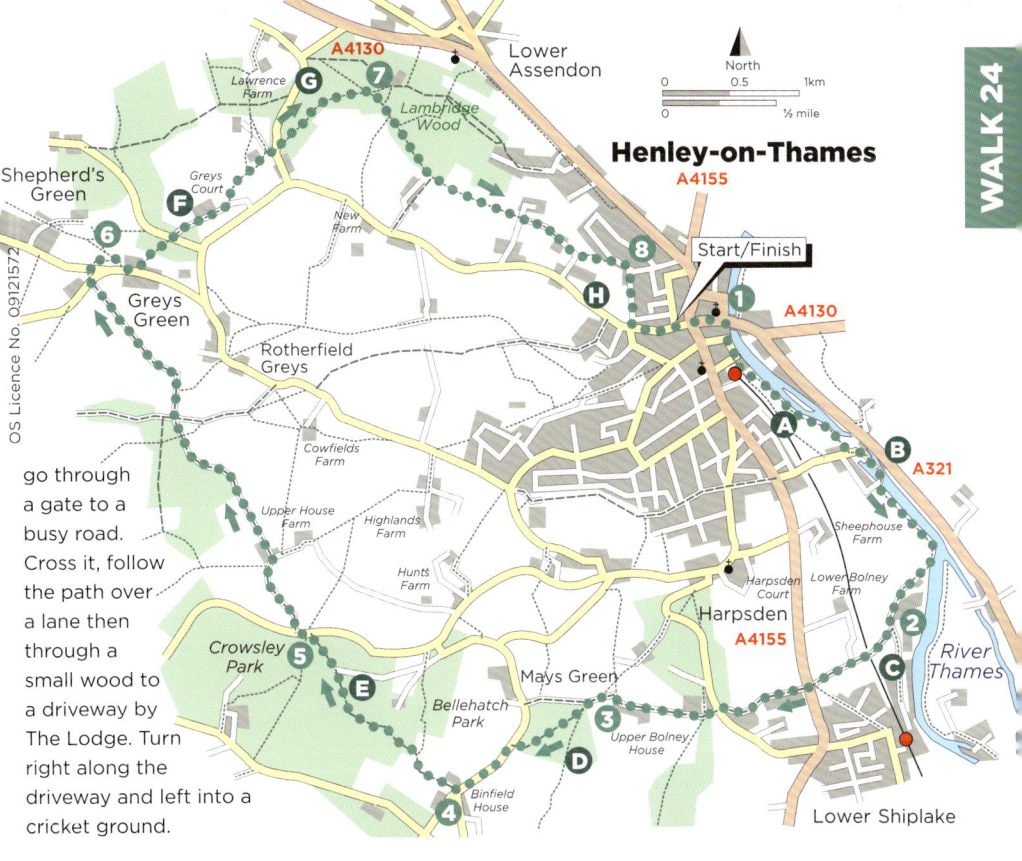

Henley-on-Thames

go through a gate to a busy road. Cross it, follow the path over a lane then through a small wood to a driveway by The Lodge. Turn right along the driveway and left into a cricket ground.

6 Cross the cricket ground heading for a path to the left of the line of cottages. Enter a wood and fork right through a gate. The path descends steeply through the next gate and into a field. Stay in the same direction, dropping down then climbing up the other side of the field. Go through a gate, cross a lane and through the next gate into the grounds of the NT's Greys Court. Turn left up the surfaced driveway, past the house on the left to the visitor entry point. Turn left immediately after it to walk through and out the back of the car park. Follow the left-hand field edge, go through two gates and turn right along the fence for 80m to a path junction where the route leaves The Chiltern Way. Stay straight ahead, go through a gate and follow the path past the farm buildings on the left to a lane. Turn right, walk towards a house and bear left on a waymarked path to a road. Bear left over the road, go through a gate and follow the path (signposted to Lower Assendon) into a

wood. Stay in the same general direction following the white arrows for nearly 1km to a crossing path.

7 Turn right for 200m to the next junction, continue ahead for a few metres and bear right downhill. Stay on the path for 600m, ignoring all other paths to left and right, to leave the wood over a low barrier onto a golf course. Go straight across following the waymark posts, and just after the 16th tee follow an avenue of trees. Go through a gate and keep straight ahead along a private driveway and a lane (Lambridge Lane).

8 Just after Croft Cottage, take the path on the left downhill to a road (Crisp Road). Turn right along it, go over Cooper Road and take the next right up Hop Gardens. Walk all the way to its junction with Gravel Hill. Turn left and follow the road down to the Town Hall, where the walk ends.

Henley-on-Thames – Town, River & Woodland

POINTS OF INTEREST

HENLEY-ON-THAMES was first recorded in 1179 when King Henry II bought land 'for the making of buildings'. A church and charter market were established in the 13th century. The historic heart of the town is around St Mary's Church (12th century), the Town Hall, Market Place and the 18th century stone bridge. There are many old buildings of special architectural or historical interest. The town is, of course, famous for its annual royal regatta and is home to many rowing clubs. Notable points of interest passed on the route are the Town Hall built to commemorate Queen Victoria's Jubilee in 1901, the old buildings in Hart Street and the church, where there's a memorial to the singer Dusty Springfield in the churchyard. In 2018, Henley-on-Thames was accredited as a Walkers Are Welcome Town.

A THE RIVER AND ROWING MUSEUM opened in 1998. It was designed by Sir David Chipperfield and was the Royal Fine Arts Commission's Building of the Year in 1999. It holds 20,000 items covering the international sport of rowing, the history of Henley-on-Thames, the story of the River Thames and an exhibition about the children's book *Wind in the Willows*.

B MARSH LOCK There has been a lock here since the early 15th century. The wooden walkway is the only one on the Thames, and was built because the lock was on the opposite bank to the towpath.

C LOWER SHIPLAKE The name probably comes from the Old English for 'stream where sheep were washed'. Another theory is that it could be named after the final resting place of a Viking ship (ship loss). There's evidence of an early settlement where cropmarks indicate prehistoric or Roman enclosures. The route passes Thameside Court, built in 1914 and currently owned by Urs Schwarzenbach, a UK-based Swiss financier, who landscaped the gardens in the early 1990s. The oldest parts of the village are towards St Peter and St Paul's Church, which dates from the 13th century.

D HIGH WOOD is part of the Phillimore Estate. Since 2015 an archaeological investigation has been undertaken by South Oxfordshire Archaeological Group. Remains have been found from the late Iron Age and throughout the Roman period. In spring there's a wonderful display of bluebells.

E CROWSLEY PARK WOOD forms part of the 160 acre Crowsley Park Estate. It's owned by the BBC and has been used as a signal-receiving station since WWII. One former owner was Henry Baskerville who's thought to have been the inspiration for Conan Doyle's *The Hound of the Baskervilles*.

F GREYS COURT takes its name from its original builders, the de Grey family. The medieval castle was fortified by the construction of a surrounding wall in 1348, from which four of the five towers and part of the wall survive. The stables and a donkey wheel house remain from an Elizabethan dwelling. The main house was destroyed in the Civil War, then rebuilt. It's now owned by the NT and is open all year round. The Chiltern Society worked with the Trust to develop walks round the estate. This project was pioneered by David Teasdale, a Society member, whose memorial gate is in the grounds.

G LAMBRIDGE WOOD is a large area of ancient beech woodland and is exceptionally rich in flora. Until 1922 it was part of the Greys Court Estate and in 1952 it became a Site of Special Scientific Interest (SSSI).

H FRIAR PARK is a late 19th century mansion with elaborate contemporary gardens and pleasure grounds designed by the original owner Frank Crisp. Later it was the home of George Harrison of The Beatles.

NEARBY CHILTERN SOCIETY WALKS

HIGHMOOR AND GREYS COURT – Walk 47 of the *50 Great Walks in the Chilterns* book meets this route near Waypoint 6.

Dorney and the River Thames on Film

WALK 25

This route will take you to see historic buildings, modern engineering projects and film locations, before finishing with a stroll along the peaceful and tranquil Thames.

LENGTH: 5.3 miles/8.6km

TERRAIN: An easy, flat walk on good paths and surfaces. The area around the footbridge after Waypoint 1 can be flooded after heavy or prolonged rain

START & FINISH: Ramblers car park, Boveney Road, Boveney SL4 6QQ. Grid ref: SU 938 777

FOOD & DRINK: Dorney Court Tea Rooms, Court Road, Dorney SL4 6QP. There are usually refreshments and toilets available at the main boathouse building just before Waypoint 6. There are two pubs off route, The Palmers Arms in Village Road and The Pineapple in Lake End Road

MAPS: OS Explorer 160

PARKING: Ramblers car park, Boveney – see above

LOCAL TRANSPORT: Bus 15 runs between Maidenhead and Slough, Monday to Saturday. There are bus stops in Eton Wick and at The Palmers Arms in Dorney. Full details can be found on www.travelinesoutheast.org.uk

Dorney Lake

Dorney and the River Thames on Film

Windsor Castle

Jubilee River

THE ROUTE

Leave by the path at the far end of the car park, go through a gate and turn left to a lane. Turn right along the lane, go over the cattle grid and past a barrier for 130m to a path on the left.

1 Turn left into a field and walk along its left-hand edge. At the end, follow the path round to the right, continue for 150m and turn left through a gap in the hedgerow. Cross the footbridge into the next field (Dorney Common). Bear right over the Common towards the left-hand end of the houses. Cross the road to the left of the cattle grid, follow the riverbank and go through the kissing gate up to a track.

2 Continue ahead, down the slope and turn left along a wide track. To the right is the Jubilee River. Stay straight ahead on this riverside track for 1.5km, go through a gate and over the car park to a busy road. Cross, turn left along the pavement and immediately right on a wide track. Continue beside the Jubilee River for a further 240m to a path junction with a bridge on the right.

3 Turn left through a gate, walk between a paddock and a field, and cross a stile to reach a road. Turn right along the pavement for 300m to the entrance to Dorney Burial Ground. Cross the road to the right of the lane to St James Church and turn right along the rough path that runs parallel to the road. At the left-hand bend, continue ahead through the entrance to Dorney Lake and walk along the wide verge to a fork in the access road.

4 *If the site is closed for an event, please follow the route opposite.* At the fork in the access road, continue straight ahead past a pair of metal barriers and through a pair of wooden gates. Follow the road round to the right, then to the left, and walk past the end of the rowing lake. Turn right up the grass slope and down through a gap into a field. Turn left to meet a surfaced track and turn left again to a path T-junction (Thames Path).

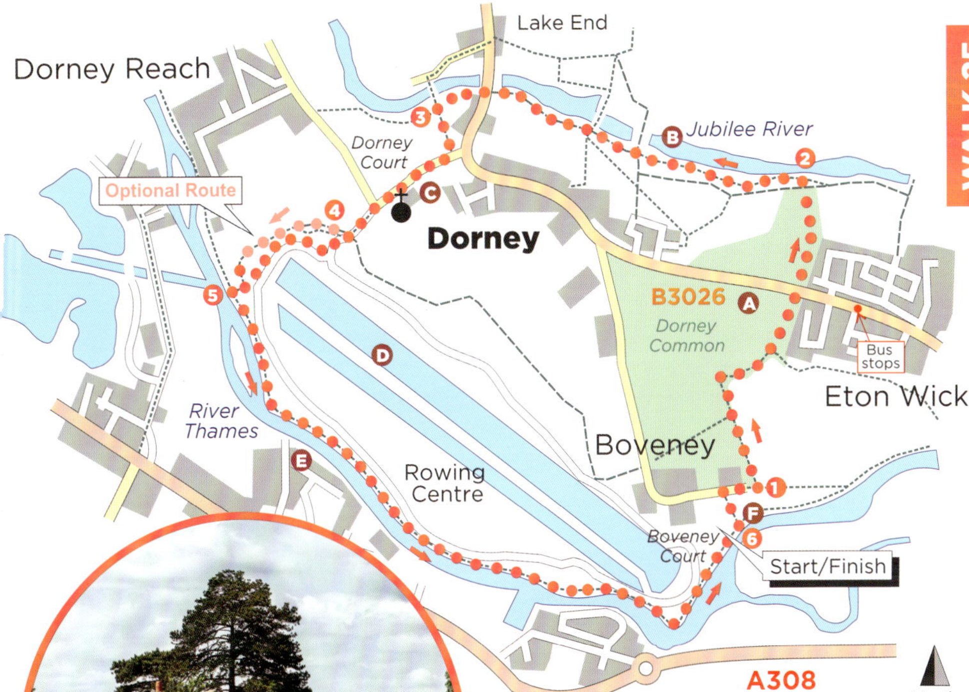

WALK 25

[Map of walking route around Dorney, Boveney, and Eton Wick]

5 Turn left and walk along the Thames riverbank for about 2.5km. Shortly after a left-hand bend, walk past the large boat house and continue for a further 230m to a path on the left.

6 Turn left along a path towards the old church of St Mary Magdalene, Boveney. After visiting it, return to the path and continue for a further 50m, then turn left through a gate to return to the car park.

ROUTE ON EVENT DAYS
Just before the fork, turn right over the access road onto a wide, surfaced track. Follow this track all the way to the Thames riverbank at Waypoint 5.

St Mary Magdalene Church

Dorney Court

Dorney and the River Thames on Film

POINTS OF INTEREST

DORNEY The name comes from the Anglo-Saxon and means 'island of bumblebees'. The Manor was mentioned in the Domesday Book, and was famed for honey. The village contains a number of cottages which date from the 17th century.

A DORNEY COMMON covers more than 169 acres and has been in agricultural use for about 1,000 years.

B JUBILEE RIVER acts as a flood relief channel for the River Thames by diverting water at peak flows. It was completed in 2001 and has been used as such on numerous occasions since. Over the years it's become a haven for wildlife, and its habitat has provided a wonderful breeding ground for birds.

C DORNEY COURT This Grade I listed house dates from the 15th century and is regarded as one of England's most beautiful Tudor manor houses. In the 16th century the estate passed to the Palmer family, who have lived there ever since. The very first pineapple to be produced in England was grown at Dorney Court and presented to Charles II in 1661. The house has been used as a film location on many occasions. Notable productions include: *A Man for All Seasons, Lock Stock and Two Smoking Barrels, The Other Boleyn Girl, Endeavour, Inspector Morse, Midsomer Murders* and *Poirot*. The Church of St James the Less is Grade I listed. It dates from the 12th century and has been the parish church since that time. It's been altered many times over the years.

D DORNEY LAKE is owned by Eton College and is set in 400 acres of parkland, with 90 acres set to water and a 100 acre nature conservation area. It had a 10 year construction programme and was opened in 2006. In 2012 it hosted the Olympic and Paralympic rowing events. The main lake is 2,200 metres long, has 8 lanes and is fed from underground aquifers. Many events take place there and, if parts of the site are closed, an alternative route is detailed on the previous page.

E RIVER THAMES The walk along the riverbank provides views of some interesting buildings on the far side. The white building is Down Place, which became Bray Film Studios after Hammer Films bought the site in 1951. Notable films were *The Quatermass Xperiment, The Curse of Frankenstein, Dracula* and *The Camp on Blood Island*. Despite being under threat of closure, filming continues to this day. Further on, the magnificent gothic structure is Oakley Court Hotel, a Grade II listed country house built in 1859. It was once the temporary home of Hammer Films before they moved to Bray. They shot five films there, including *The Man in Black*. After Hammer left, the house was still used as a film set for many productions, such as *Half a Sixpence* and *The Rocky Horror Picture Show*.

F ST MARY MAGDALENE CHURCH A church has stood on this site since before the Norman Conquest. The present Grade I listed church dates from the 12th century, and was a chapel-of-ease to St Peter's, Burnham. It served the bargees who shipped timber downriver, and became known as 'the bargees' church'. It was transferred to Eton parish in 1911, declared redundant in 1975 and threatened with demolition. It passed into the care of the Friends of Friendless Churches in 1983.